European Foundation
for the Improvement of
Living and Working Conditions

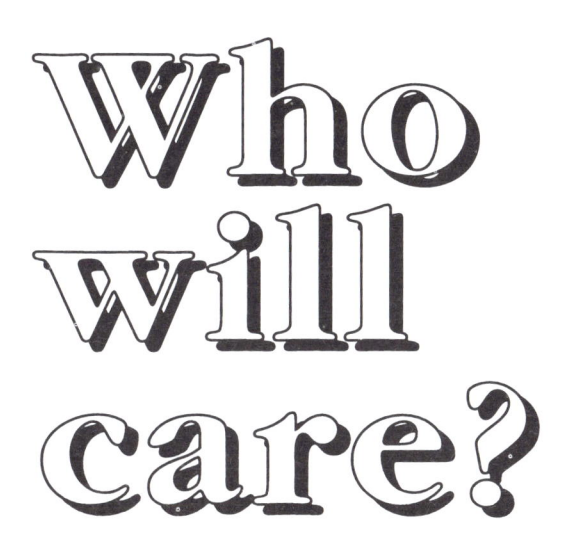

Who will care?

Future prospects for family care of older people in the European Union

EF/95/25/EN

Ann Salvage is a medical sociologist with a special interest in old age. She prepared this report as a Research Associate at the Age Concern Institute of Gerontology, King's College London, and previously spent five years as a Research Officer with the Research Team for the Care of the Elderly, University of Wales College of Medicine in Cardiff. Her previous work has included evaluation studies of services for elderly people and a national survey of elderly people in cold weather.

The Age Concern Institute of Gerontology (ACIOG) at King's College, University of London, was established in 1986 as a joint venture with Age Concern England. Under the direction of Professor Anthea Tinker, the Institute undertakes a wide variety of gerontological research and offers a Ph.D programme and M.Sc. course in Gerontology. The Institute publishes books and reports, holds conferences, seminars and public lectures on aspects of ageing and is active in the development of international links and cross-national research.

European Foundation
for the Improvement of
Living and Working Conditions

Who will care?

Future prospects for family care of older people in the European Union

Ann V. Salvage

Loughlinstown House,
Shankill, Co. Dublin, Ireland
Tel.: (+353) 1 282 6888 Fax: (+353) 1 282 6456

Cataloguing data can be found at the end of this publication

Luxembourg: Office for Official Publications of the European Communities, 1995

ISBN 92-827-5360-3

© European Foundation for the Improvement of Living and Working Conditions, 1995

For rights of translation or reproduction, applications should be made to the Director, European Foundation for the Improvement of Living and Working Conditions, Loughlinstown House, Shankill, Co. Dublin, Ireland.

Printed in Ireland

SUMMARY

Introduction: The most significant demographic phenomenon uniting the European Union (EU) Member States today is the ageing of their populations; it has been estimated that, between 1991 and 2015, the numbers of people in the EU aged 60 and over will increase by 4m. The future care of elderly people is a subject of serious concern for all Member States and represents part of the on-going debate about family responsibilities, family values and policy on the family.

Aims: In the context of growing concern over the future availability and willingness of families to care for their elderly relatives, this report aims to inform the debate on the question of who will provide care for elderly people in the future. Looking ahead to the year 2014, it considers the likely future demand for and supply of family care for elderly people.

Influences on the future demand for care: Factors which will influence future demand for care include: demographic factors (e.g. fertility and mortality rates), disability and health, elderly people's preferences for care and their incomes and political power.

The numbers of elderly people (in particular people aged 80 and over) will continue to increase, and although the physical health of elderly people in the future is difficult to predict, the incidence of dementia is likely to increase substantially with significant implications for care provision. Elderly people's living standards appear to be generally on the increase, but polarisation between those without occupational or private pensions is likely to perpetuate current disparities in choice of care. As they come to represent an increasing proportion of the European electorate, however, it is likely that elderly people in the future will be more vociferous in expressing their wishes in relation to care provision.

Influences on the future supply of care: The level of availability of family care in the Europe of the future will depend not only on families' *ability* to provide care (which will be affected by the female employment rate, divorce rates, carers' health, service and financial support and child care demands) but also on their *willingness* to provide care. It will also depend on the availability of alternative care sources and on public policies and ideologies.

Although there is no evidence that families are no longer willing to care for their elderly relatives, from the second decade of the "next generation" women (who represent a high proportion of carers) in relation to the numbers of elderly people likely to need care. Increasing divorce rates and any increases in female employment could further reduce the availability of family carers.

Conclusions and options for the future: Among the elderly populations of the future, elderly women will be especially at risk of neglect, for many of them are likely to be widowed, to have high dependency needs, and to be living alone on low incomes. Also at risk will be those who, without occupational or private pensions, are not able to purchase the care they need and must rely on an overburdened welfare state or on their families for care. The chances of large increases in formal service provision appear very low. If factors with the potential to increase demand for care exert their maximum effects in combination with factors reducing the supply of care we will be faced, in 20 years time, with a "crisis" of care unlike anything in Europe has experiences in the past.

There is an urgent need for the governments of the Member States to recognise just how much they currently depend on informal carers - many of whom are themselves elderly - and to consider all possible options in making solid plans for the future. The report presents four "options" which may be considered in approaching the issue of future care for elderly people:

a) **Reducing demand for care: a preventive approach:** This strategy would attempt to reduce the demand for care by focusing on improving elderly people's health and independence.

b) **Stimulating supply: supporting carers:** This approach would focus on making it easier for families to provide care for elderly relatives and considering their needs alongside those of dependants.

c) **Alternative approaches to care in the community:** This would involve thinking beyond existing structures towards other ways in which care needs could be met.

d) **A new face for institutional care?** Antipathy to institutional care is based on individual's perceptions of particular *forms* of institutional care, and the development of alternative forms could alter the perceptions of tomorrow's elderly people to the extent that they enter individual consciousness as desirable and accessible options.

This report will add impctus and focus to the debate on the family care of elderly people in the EU, and will be of interest to policy makers, workers in the "caring" profession, informal carers, researchers and elderly people themselves.

CONTENTS

	Page
Foreword	1
Introduction: Elderly People in Europe. Family Care in Context	3
Shared challenges in the European Union	3
The future of family care	4
The nature of "futures" studies	5
Aims	6
Chapter 1: Conceptualising Care. Models and Definitions	8
Development of a conceptual model	8
Definitional issues	9
Chapter 2: The Potential Demand for Family Care	12
The concept of "demand"	12
Influences on the future demand for care	12
The ageing of Europe	13
Causes of population ageing	14
More women than men	15
Population projections	16
Disability and health: present and future	17
The challenge of dementia	21
Routes to independence? Housing and technology	21
What do elderly people want? Attitudes, preferences and choice	22
How will preferences change?	25
Political/Economic factors	26
Elderly people's incomes	28
Trends in retirement and pensions	30
Political power	31
Summary: The potential demand for family care of elderly people	33
Chapter 3: The Potential Supply of Family Care for Older People	34
Family care: alive and well	34
Influences on the future supply of care	34
Caring in the 90s: who are the carers?	35

Carers: ability to provide care		37
Changes in fertility rates		37
Remarriage and divorce		38
Competing demands? Child care and employment		41
Childcare		41
Female employment		42
Health: future prospects for carers		44
Service and financial support		44
Migration		45
Carers: willingness to provide care		46
Intergenerational relationships		46
Attitudes to giving care		47
Motivations: why do carers care?		48
How far will they go? The limits to caring		50
Support needs		51
Employment and caring: choice or balance?		51
Employment or caring: is there a conflict?		52
Carers and employment: looking to the future		53
Available options: alternative sources of care		55
The balance of service provision: public, private and voluntary		55
Policy and ideology		57
Policies for the future?		58
Economic factors		60
Recession and the search for cheaper care		60
Competing demands for resources		61
The effect of the 'unpredictable'		62
Summary: the potential supply of family care for elderly people		63
Chapter 4: Conclusions and Options for the Future		65
Conclusions		65
Options for the future		68
Reducing demand for care: a preventive approach		69
Stimulating supply: supporting carers		71
Alternative approaches to Care in the Community		75
A new face for institutional care?		76
References		77
Appendix 1: National Reports		87

FOREWORD

The research on which this report is based was part of the fourth four-year rolling programme of the European Foundation for the Improvement of Living and Working Conditions which ran from 1989 to 1992 (European Foundation, 1989). Researchers in eleven of the European Union (EU) Member States prepared reports on the experiences of people caring for an elderly relative (for details of these reports see Appendix 1) and a consolidated report, drawing together information from the national reports, was produced (Jani-Le Bris, 1993a).

In November 1993, The Age Concern Institute of Gerontology (ACIOG), Kings College London, was asked to compile a report on future prospects for the family care of elderly people in the European Union, to be based on the information contained in the eleven Member States' reports and documentation from a wide range of official sources.

The work was undertaken at ACIOG between November 1993 and February 1994. An International Workshop to discuss the draft report, held in London on the 4th February 1994, was attended by experts from nine European Member States.

The author would like to thank Robert Anderson (European Foundation), and the grant holders - Professor Anthea Tinker (ACIOG) and Dr Janet Askham (ACIOG) - for their invaluable advice and assistance.

INTRODUCTION: ELDERLY PEOPLE IN EUROPE - FAMILY CARE IN CONTEXT

Shared Challenges in the European Union

The twelve Member States comprising the European Union in 1994 differ from one another on many social and economic dimensions; Qvortup has noted that "for some, talking about Europe would be an impossible abstraction" (Qvortup, 1989:20). As Qvortup goes on to observe, however, in a number of sociologically relevant respects, Europe can be regarded as an entity. "Compared with other parts of the world Europe is a continent whose similarities are more conspicuous than the differences between its countries. Demographically, economically, educationally and socially it distinguishes itself, together with other industrialised countries, from those of the Third World, but at the same time the history of Europe sets it apart from other industrialised countries outside Europe." (ibid).

The recent Green Paper on European Social Policy (Commission of the European Communities, 1993a) identifies a number of major social trends and challenges for Europe, but the most significant demographic phenomenon uniting the European Member States today is the ageing of their populations. In 1991 there were 68,576,000 people aged 60 and over in the European Union; by the year 2015, it is estimated that there will be an extra 14 million people aged 60 and over in the Union, of whom 4 million will be aged 80 or over (Eurostat, 1991: Table I-5; Eurostat, 1993a: Table B-2). All European Union countries are experiencing similar demographic change: lower fertility rates coupled with higher life expectancy - although they have different starting points. There is considerable convergence between Member States in the proportion of their populations aged 65 and over (Walker, 1992). Table 1 shows how the proportion of elderly people in the European Union countries is likely to change between 1990 and 2020.

As we move towards a new century, the care of elderly people is a subject of serious social and economic concern for all Member States and represents part of the on-going debate about family responsibilities, family values and policy on the family. This debate focuses on questions such as whether or not families will be able and/or willing to care for elderly relatives in the future, to what extent they can and should be expected to provide care, and whether individual Member States can - or should - rovide services for all elderly people.

The Future of Family Care

A number of trends may be identified as contributing to the current concern over the future care of elderly people:

(a) <u>Demographic Changes</u>

The numbers and proportion of elderly people in the European Union are increasing, and will continue to increase, over the next 20 years. The most rapid increase has been, and will continue to be, in the proportion of very elderly people who are the heaviest consumers of health and social services. Many of those providing care are the elderly husbands and wives of dependent elderly people.

(b) <u>Changes in the Structure of the Family</u>

Smaller families, increases in the number of young people who live together rather than marrying, increased divorce and re-marriage rates and geographical mobility are considered to reduce the potential availability of family members to care for frail elderly people.

(c) <u>The Employment of Women</u>

The increasing entry of women into the labour force in Europe raises questions concerning the likely availability of women (who represent the majority of the informal caring population) to care for elderly relatives.

(d) <u>Financial Restrictions</u>

A major societal change is the economic recession and the retrenchment and redefinition of the whole system of social welfare which has taken place in most western European countries since the late 1970s (Bak, 1989). There have been moves towards cost containment in spending on health and social services and concern is being expressed about the ability of the welfare state to support the increasing numbers of elderly people in the future.

(e) <u>Humanistic Concerns</u>

Coincident with these changes has been the growth of concern over issues such as individual rights, citizenship and the quality of life (Glendinning and McLaughlin, 1993). In this context questions are being raised about the acceptability of current levels of family responsibility for the care of older people in terms of the quality of life of family carers.

There is a concern in all European Union Member States about the cost implications of population ageing (in terms of pensions and health and social services). At the same time there is increasing attention to quality of life issues, with the social, psychological and emotional costs of caring coming more into focus. A popular conception has developed that the availability of informal carers in Europe will decline in the future due to lower fertility rates, changes in the structure of the family and the employment of women, but the overall effect of the changes mentioned above has not been carefully analysed. With diversity of awareness and provision across the European Union, there has been a failure to develop a comprehensive vision of the situation, and limited debate has taken place based on relatively unchallenged assumptions. It was the need to look more closely at the effects and interactions of social, economic and other trends which prompted the research on which this report is based.

The Nature of "Futures" Studies

This report may be regarded as a "Futures Study" (Secretariat for Futures Studies, 1978). As a Swedish commentary on such studies has observed, it may be argued that, strictly speaking "One cannot study an event which has not yet occurred and that futures studies are therefore impossible" (op cit: 67). If, however, one regards them as "studies with the future *in prospect*" (ibid) the approach becomes easier to accept. Futures studies have been described as studies of society which have a long time perspective and have the following aims:

- To watch over the long term changes in society.
- To describe alternative possibilities of development
- To discuss problems that embrace several sectors
- To stimulate problem-oriented and interdisciplinary research (op cit: 68).

Another aim of the work undertaken at the Swedish Secretariat for Futures Studies is "to contribute material to the political discussions on the design of the future society." This is based on the idea that "the future is not predetermined but can be influenced; by presenting a basis for the political discussions on the future, the standard of knowledge of, and involvement in, these issues may be increased." (op cit: 69).

Aims

The broad aim of this report is to inform the debate (at both national and European levels) on the question of who will provide care for dependent elderly people in the future. While being aimed particularly at policy makers in public, private and voluntary sectors, it should be of interest to a number of other audiences including workers in the "caring" professions, informal carers, researchers and elderly people themselves.

Bearing in mind the recommendations of the Swedish Secretariat for Futures Studies that the time perspective of such studies "must be long enough for the conditions studied to be influenceable but not so long that the question ceases to be of importance in current decisions and planning", a time perspective of the next twenty years was adopted. (Of course, the available data and projections adopt various time perspectives. Information across a large range of trends and changes has been drawn upon with an emphasis upon international comparative sources; so, for example, demographic projections for the year 2015 were utilised since these were readily available from Eurostat.)

Table 1: The older population in 1990 and 2020 as a percentage of the total population

		B	DK	D	GR	E	F	IRL	I	L	NL	P	UK	EUR 12
1990	50+	32.0	30.8	34.1	32.8	29.6	29.7	23.6	32.4	31.1	27.4	29.2	31.2	31.3
	60+	20.4	20.3	20.8	19.4	18.5	19.1	15.1	20.2	19.1	17.2	18.2	20.7	19.7
	65+	14.7	15.5	15.3	13.7	13.2	14.0	11.3	14.4	13.3	12.8	13.2	15.6	14.4
	75+	6.6	6.9	7.4	6.0	5.4	6.8	4.4	6.3	6.0	5.3	5.3	6.8	6.5
	85+	1.4	1.4	1.4	1.0	1.0	1.5	0.7	1.1	1.1	1.1	0.8	1.5	1.3
2020	50+	43.5	40.4	47.1	40.2	41.1	39.5	36.5	46.8	42.0	40.5	41.0	38.0	42.2
	60+	28.2	25.8	29.7	26.0	24.9	26.1	22.9	29.9	26.8	25.2	25.5	23.9	26.7
	65+	20.8	19.5	22.2	19.9	18.3	19.7	16.6	22.8	19.3	18.6	18.8	27.6	20.0
	75+	9.1	8.2	10.6	9.2	7.9	8.2	6.1	10.7	8.2	7.4	8.7	12.4	8.9
	85+	2.8	2.0	2.5	5.5	2.1	2.4	1.3	2.8	2.1	1.9	2.8	3.6	2.4

Note: 1991 data incomplete

Source: Walker et al., (1993:13) from Eurostat statistics

CHAPTER ONE: CONCEPTUALISING CARE. MODELS AND DEFINITIONS

The Development of a Conceptual Model

Since the debate on the future of family care for older people is frequently framed in terms of 'demand' and 'supply' (the issues of how much care will be needed and of whether that care will be available), the analyses in this paper adopt a 'demand - supply' framework (Figure 1). Using this framework, it was possible to consider likely future changes in terms of:

- Extent and level of care which would be required in the future
- Potential availability of family care to meet this demand.

The supply/demand model used here is to a large extent a "construct of convenience" and does not conform strictly to economic models. There is much potential for interaction within the model, with some variables having concurrent effects upon both supply and demand (thus, for instance, traditional family care practices will influence both the preparedness of carers to support elderly people and the readiness of elderly people to accept care). The model is "impure" to the extent that one cannot always necessarily assume causality within it: supply and demand are not always related in the ways one would expect.

Three over-arching concepts have been incorporated into the framework:

Uniformity/Diversity

The twelve Member States of the European Union, while they are experiencing similar demographic trends, vary considerably in terms of many of the variables discussed in this paper. One of the most obvious dimensions of diversity, for instance, is the extent to which families are required by the state to provide support for elderly people. Another is the level and type (public, private or voluntary) of service provision. The analysis has sought to be sufficiently sensitive to incorporate these differences between Member States at the same time as considering their similarities.

Predictability/Unpredictability

For very few, if any, of the variables considered is it possible to project ahead with full confidence. Probably the most reliable are the demographic projections - the likely number and age balance of elderly people and the corresponding numbers of potential informal carers in the future. Even these - based as they are on assumptions about fertility and (more importantly for this study) mortality and migration - are not by any means totally reliable, but they are probably a lot easier to predict than, say, changes in attitudes to giving or receiving care.

Dependency and Interdependency

Many of the informal carers discussed in this report will themselves be elderly people - either elderly spouses or elderly children caring for their very elderly parents. To avoid the interpretation of what is happening in Europe in a way which defines care of elderly people as "a problem" or elderly populations as "a burden", the notions of exchange and reciprocity should be kept very much in mind.

Definitional Issues

In the earlier national reports prepared for the European Foundation (see Appendix 1) two basic definitions were adhered to in order to ensure comparability:

"Family Carer"

A family carer was defined as "a person who is related to the person he or she is caring for either by blood or by marriage" (Jani-Le Bris, 1993a: 4). This definition was itself based on the definition of the family as "a succession of individuals who are descended from each other, and those who are related to them by marriage" (Jani-Le Bris, 1993: 4), which may be distinguished from the tighter concept of the "nuclear family" comprising the unit "based on a marriage and parenthood" (Finch, 1989: 83).

"Care"

"Family care" for elderly people may take many different forms: families may, for example, provide emotional, financial, practical or physical support. The earlier European Foundation national reports examined support provided for physically frail elderly people. In this report, emphasis is also placed on the implications for care of the likely increase in the numbers of mentally frail elderly people.

Figure 1: Family Care in the Balance
Level of Provision of Family Care for Elderly People
depends on

Demand Factors

Number of elderly people in need of care
Depends on:

Demographic factors
Fertility rates
Mortality rates
Migration rates
Household situation
Sex-balance

Disability/Health
Physical/mental health
Preventive health/health behaviour
Ameliorative care

Preferences/Choice
Intergenerational relations
Traditions/expectations
Attitudes to institutions
Exchange and reciprocity
Notions of independence/self-determination

Political/Economic Factors
Political power of elderly people

Purchasing power (incomes/pensions)

Aids to Independence
Assistive technology
Housing

Uniformity/Diversity

Dependency/Interdependency

Predictability/Unpredictability

Supply Factors

Number of carers available
Depends on:
Carers: Ability/Opportunity
Fertility rates/child-care
Effects of divorce/remarriage
Migration/geographical proximity
Physical/psychological health
Service/financial support
Workforce participation
Child-care demands

Carers: Willingness/Motivation
Intergenerational relationships
Attitudes to provision of care/traditions
Desire for employment
Support needs

Alternative Care Sources
Level/balance of state/voluntary/private domiciliary/institutional care
Provision of housing

Public Policies/Ideologies
Policies re: family/state obligations
Financial support for elderly people/carers

Economic Factors
Economic growth/recession
Competing financial demands

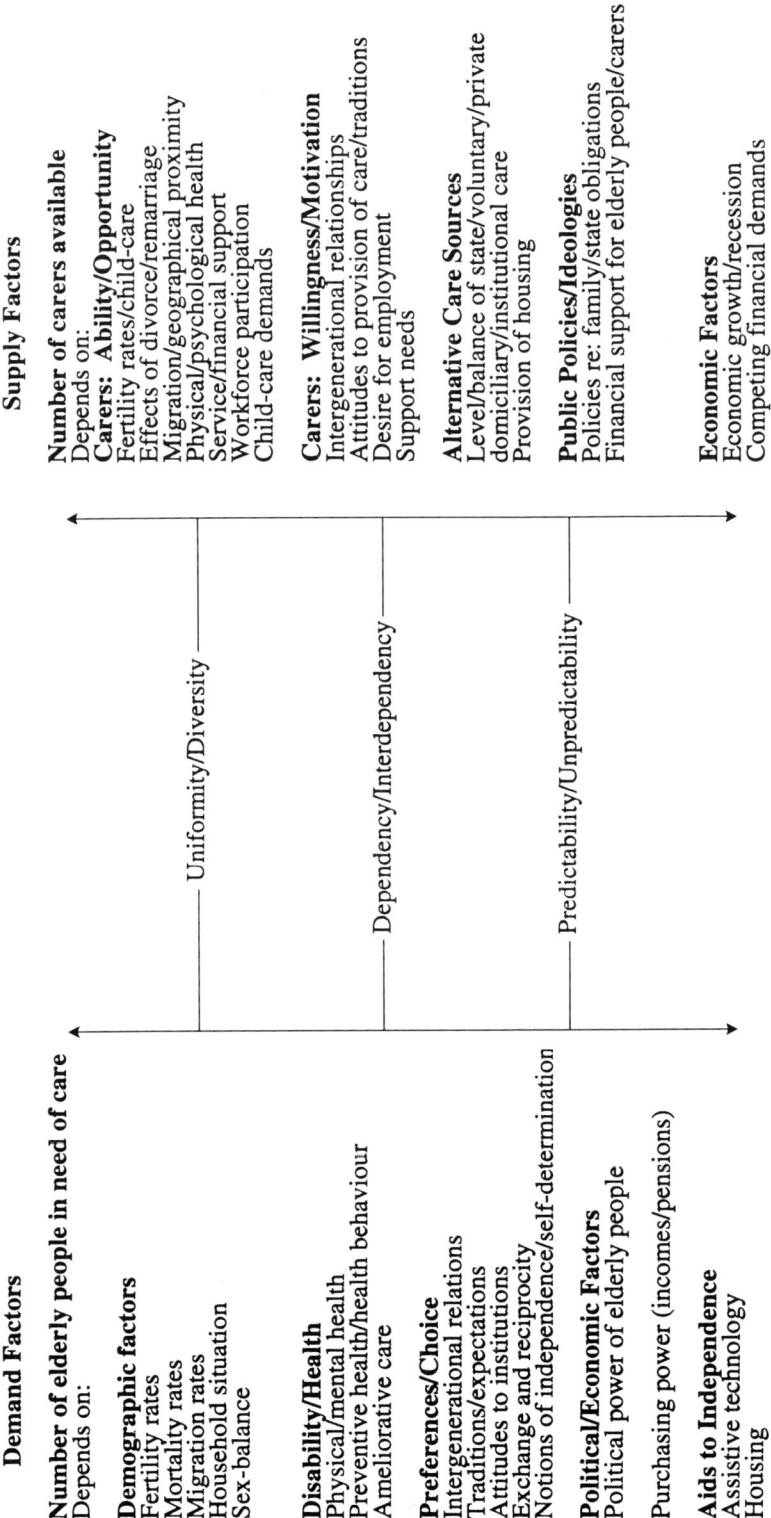

10

"Elderly People"

Although not all countries were able to provide information solely concerning this age group the definition of elderly people adopted for the purposes of the earlier European Foundation reports was those "over the age of 74" (Jani-Le Bris, 1993a: 4). The current report adopts a wider definition - commonly used in gerontological research. In this document the term "elderly people" refers essentially to people aged 60 and over, but again the focus is upon dependent people in need of care and support.

CHAPTER TWO: THE POTENTIAL DEMAND FOR FAMILY CARE

The Concept of "Demand"

Since it is intended to utilise what has been described as a "supply/demand" model there is a clear need to define at an early stage what is meant by the terms of supply and demand. While the concept of supply of care is relatively unproblematic, that of demand is less clear cut. Should one talk about "articulated" demand for care (in terms of what people actually ask for)? Should the word refer to "latent" demand for care (in terms of assumed correspondences between physical or psychological conditions and need for assistance?). Should the discussion be based on people's *perceived needs*? Evers has observed that, "it is a long and complicated process to translate objectivated needs perceived into articulated demands." (Evers 1992: 2). In analysing the potential demand for family care, therefore, the discussion will encompass not only factors which have the potential to affect objective *need for care* in the future (e.g. how many dependent elderly people there are likely to be) but also what elderly people are likely to *expect* and *want* in terms of family support.

Influences on the Future Demand for Care

Adopting the "wide" definition of demand described above, a number of factors suggest themselves for discussion. Firstly, the overall numbers of elderly people would need to be taken into account, using population projections.

Since our concern is with the numbers and proportion of elderly people who will need assistance in the future, likely changes in disability and health will have to be considered. It will obviously be necessary to take account of not only current health and disability levels in elderly populations and variations by age, but also of factors that will have a potential to improve or worsen these aspects. Preventive health care and changes in health behaviour are among the most important factors which have the potential to reduce illness, but developments in technology also have potential for making it easier for elderly people to remain in their own homes and able to rely less on care from others. The incidence of dementia increases with increasing age, and is a particularly difficult problem for family carers, so it will be necessary to look at the implications of an ageing population for changes in incidence of this type of illness.

Moving from relatively "objective" factors which are likely to affect demand for care to more "subjective" criteria, an important element on the demand side will be older people's attitudes towards and expectations of care. What, if anything, do they want or expect their families to do for them? How - if at all - is this likely to change in the future?

Finally, there is a need to consider elderly people's *power*, both in terms of political/pressure group power and of purchasing power. This involves looking at what is happening in the Member States in terms of elderly people's co-operative activity and organisation and at their current and likely future financial position.

The Ageing of Europe

The populations of the Member States of the European Union are ageing; that is to say that the proportion of elderly people in their populations is increasing and will continue to increase into the next century. In 1991, 13.6% of the population of the European Union was aged 65 or more - while 18.2% of the population was aged less than 15 years (Eurostat, 1993a: Table D-3).

Because of variations in fertility, mortality and migration rates among Member States, population ageing varies across the European Union, with countries in the North and West of the community (with the exception of Ireland) having the oldest populations and those in the South the youngest (Table 2).

Of particular concern today is the increasing proportion of very elderly people in the European population; since these are the people who are most likely to make demands on family and care services their growing numbers have significant implications for policy in the European Union. In 1991, there were 11,937,000 people aged 80 and over in the European Union (Eurostat, 1993: Table B-9), representing 3.5% of the total European Union population and 15% of the population aged 60 and over. This proportion will increase in the future (see "Population Projections").

Table 2: Proportion of the population aged 60+ and 80+: European Union, 1991

	60+ %	80+ %
Belgium	20.7	3.5
Denmark	20.3	3.7
France	19.3	3.8
Germany	20.4	3.8
Greece[1]	20.2	3.2
Ireland	15.3	2.2
Italy	20.6	3.3
Luxembourg	19.1	3.1
Netherlands	17.4	2.9
Portugal	18.3	2.5
Spain	18.9	2.9
UK	20.7	3.7
(EUR.12)	**19.9**	**3.5**

[1] Provisional data.

Source: Eurostat, 1993a: Table B-12

Causes of Population Ageing

Changes in the age structure of a population are determined by trends in fertility, mortality and internal migration. By far the most important determinant of population age structure in Europe has been past and current fertility trends (birth rates) (Grundy and Harrop, 1992a). In 1960, the total fertility rate (average number of children born per woman) was 2.61 in Europe. By 1974 this had fallen to 2.08 and by 1991 to 1.51 (Eurostat, 1993: Table E-1). Trends in mortality are also important in determining age structure. Historically, falls in mortality generally served partially to offset the trends towards an older population, since it was falls in infant mortality which were most marked (Grundy and Harrop, 1992a). However, while in the past it was fertility trends which were pre-eminent in shaping the age structures of populations, the situation in many European countries today is rather different. In much of today's Europe, birth and death rates are low, the proportions of elderly people high, and most deaths occur among those aged 65 or more. Grundy and Harrop observe that "in these circumstances trends in mortality, particularly at older ages, become the major determinant of *further* population ageing, including the ageing of the elderly population itself" (Grundy and Harrop, 1992a: 19).

The steady rise in life expectancy resulting from progress in medical science and improved living conditions is responsible for the large increases in the numbers of elderly people in the European Union (Commission of the European Communities, 1993b). In 1960, life expectancy at birth for men in the European Union was 67.3 years - by 1991 this had risen to 72.8. The equivalent figures for women were 72.7 and 78.0 (Eurostat 1993: Table G22).

More Women than Men

The variation between male and female life expectancy in the European Union has considerable consequences for old people (Commission of the European Communities, 1993b). In the 60-64 year age group there are roughly the same numbers of men and women but with increasing age, the imbalance between the sexes increases so that in the 80 to 84 year old group there are two women to every man and in the 90 to 94 year old group the ratio is three to one (op cit). Table 3 shows how the ratio of men and women varied by age group for the 12 Member States in 1990. The fact that there are many more elderly (and particularly very elderly) women in the population of the European Union has significant implications for care, since elderly women tend to suffer higher levels of disability than men of the same age (Martin, Meltzer & Elliot, 1988). Elderly women are more likely to be widowed than men, more likely to live alone, and more likely to have low incomes (Dooghe, 1993: 3).

Population Projections

How will the structure of the population of the European Union change over the next 20 years? The reliability of population projections depends on the accuracy of the assumptions on which they are based and the sensitivity of the projections to variations in the assumptions (OECD, 1988). Changes in fertility are very difficult to predict but, since we are looking 20 years ahead and are mainly interested in the likely number of elderly people and potential carers (mainly elderly people and middle-aged women), we can consider projections for these groups to be relatively free of bias from this source (Dooghe, 1993: 3). Mortality assumptions are generally considered more reliable than fertility assumptions in the short and medium term, but the main potential for future change is at the upper end of the age range, with the possibility that further reductions in mortality at older ages will accelerate the ageing of populations (op cit).

In 1991 there were 68,576,000 people aged 60 and over in the European Union (including 11,936,000 aged 80 or more). By 2015, Eurostat projections suggest that there will be an extra 14 million people aged 60 or more including an extra 4 million aged 80 and over (Eurostat, 1991: Table I-5; Eurostat, 1993a: Table B-2). (We can be relatively confident of the accuracy of these figures; given that they are based on numbers of people already born.) Based on these estimates a quarter of the European Union population would then be aged 60 or over (Eurostat, 1991: Table I-5).

Table 3: Proportion of the population in elderly age groups, sex ratios (males per 100 females) of the elderly population and numbers aged 65 and over, EC countries, 1990

	% aged			Sex ratio (m/fx100)			No. aged 65+ (000s)
	65-74	75-84	85+	65-74	75+	65+	
Belgium	8.2	5.3	1.4	79	51	65	1474
Denmark	8.6	5.4	1.5	82	57	70	800
France	7.2	5.3	1.6	78	52	64	7882
Germany	7.9	6.0	1.4	60	44	52	9614
Greece	7.6	5.0	1.1	82	72	77	1374
Ireland	6.8	3.7	0.8	85	64	76	397
Italy	8.2	5.1	1.2	76	56	67	8336
Luxembourg	7.4	4.9	1.2	66	48	58	51
Netherlands	7.4	4.2	1.2	78	52	66	1906
Portugal	7.8	4.5	0.9	78	58	69	1359
Spain	7.8	4.4	1.1	78	58	69	5161
UK	8.7	5.4	1.5	81	52	66	8967
EUR 12	**8.0**	**5.2**	**1.3**	**75**	**52**	**64**	**44333**

Source: Eurostat, 1991 (in Grundy & Harrop 1993:17)

Disability and Health: Present and Future

The major concern in looking ahead to likely future demand, is not the sheer *numbers* of elderly people who will be living in the European Union, but how many of them will need help - whether from families or other sources. Attempting to address this question is by no means straightforward; one cannot simply extrapolate from current disability rates using projected future numbers of elderly people. To begin with, population projections themselves make assumptions about mortality rates which can be influenced by a number of factors.

The vast majority of today's population of elderly people in the European Union are fit, active and able to live independently (Eurolink Age, 1993a; Walker, 1993). Although only a small proportion of the population 60 and over need help with activities of daily living, however, disability and dependency do increase with increasing age (Walker et al., 1993). Assessing dependency levels across the European Union as a whole is difficult, since few representative national surveys have been conducted in the Member States and those which have been undertaken adopt different measures of dependency (Jani-Le Bris, 1993a).

One study which did address the question of dependency at a European level found that just under two-fifths (38%) of the population aged 60 and over said that they were suffering from functional incapacity (Walker, 1993). The variations were quite wide between countries, from 53% in Greece to 22% in Belgium, suggesting that, apart from 'true' differences, some variation may have occurred in the interpretation of the question. Predictably however, there was an association between age and disability: 32% of those aged 60 to 64 reported a limiting long standing illness or disability compared with 47% of those aged 80 and over (op cit). Table 4 shows the proportion of different age groups receiving regular assistance from spouses and public services for the European Union as a whole.

Table 4: Proportion of different age groups receiving regular help or assistance from spouses and the public services

	60-64	65-69	70-74	75-79	80+
Spouse	54%	44%	33%	25%	16%
Public services	8%	8%	10%	13%	20%

Source: Walker (1993:28)

The European study also asked elderly people about the care that they were receiving (if any). Here the focus was on regular assistance with personal care and household tasks with which people needed help because they found it difficult to do them by themselves. Again there were large differences between age groups, with 18% of 60 to 64 year olds saying they had regular assistance with personal care or household tasks compared with 59% of those aged 80 and over (op cit). Asking about the help people actually receive cannot, of course, indicate accurately the number of people who consider themselves to need help (quite apart from objective measures of dependency). Neither can it elucidate the actual frequency and intensity of assistance required. What is clear however is that while many elderly people remain able to care for themselves, increasing age brings increasing need for help and assistance. Of particular significance is the fact that the rate of disability among women is higher than that among men (Martin, Meltzer & Elliot, 1988). With increasing numbers of women living into very old age in the future this could have significant implications for care. Many of these elderly women will be living alone, and with relatively high levels of dependency (compared with younger women), their needs for practical, physical and nursing care are likely to be high.

Jani-Le Bris (1993a) notes that research from a number of northern European countries points to a general improvement in the health of elderly populations over the past few years. In looking to the future, however, account must be taken of the differential increases which are occurring in life expectancy, on the one hand, and in "disability free" life expectancy on the other. An American study has shown that, between 1970 and 1980, 'disability-free' life expectancy increased at a lower rate than general life expectancy (Crimmins *et al.*, 1989). Although there is no consensus (Dooghe, 1993), the chances are high that in the next twenty years, any increase in life expectancy will mean longer periods of disability and dependency for elderly people.

Fries (1980, 1989) has argued that, throughout the twentieth century, people have been living longer, with incapacity delayed to a greater age and compressed into fewer years before death, and with elderly people therefore staying active and healthy longer than they used to. A controversial assumption of the 'compression of morbidity' thesis, however, is that there is a natural limit to the life-span. Manton (1982), for instance, has argued that there is no evidence of a 'natural' upper limit to the life-span.

Estimating the number of elderly people who will require assistance in the future is hindered by our incomplete knowledge of current levels of dependency in Europe and uncertainties concerning the likely future relationship between changes in life expectancy and changes in disability free life expectancy. It is also restricted by the fact that it is not possible to predict with any level of accuracy the effects of factors which could improve the health and independence of elderly people. Increases in life expectancy among younger and older people, as well as the advances in medicine since the turn of the century, have led to the older members of the European Union using an increasing level of medical care (Hafner, 1986). This paradox derives from the fact that antibiotics and vaccines, for example, reduce the mortality risk but increase the risk of chronic illnesses against which medicine is largely ineffective in curative terms and from which people were saved until recently by early death (Jani-Le Bris, 1993a). The most significant health problems among elderly people are cardiovascular complaints (which, numerically, head both the cause of death and morbidity statistics in Europe), malignant tumours, psychological illnesses, diseases of the skeletal system (arthritis, osteoporosis) and respiratory tract diseases (op cit and Eurostat, 1993b).

Various estimates have been made of the increase in life expectancy which would occur should significant improvements in the treatment or elimination of circulatory diseases or cancer be achieved (DaneAge, N/D; Dooghe, 1992). However, since a relatively short period of time (20 years) is under consideration here, it is possible that the strongest potential influences upon the incidence of these diseases will be changes in lifestyle and behaviour, rather than medical breakthroughs.

The US Public Health Service has estimated that lifestyle accounts for nearly two fifths to more than one half of the mortality from heart disease, cancer, cerebrovascular disease and arteriosclerosis (US Public Health Service, 1978). There is evidence that many health changes that are common in old age are more the result of earlier and/or current exposure to various risks than of the biological process of ageing (Healthy Ageing, 1990: 16). Healthy lifestyles, as Dooghe observes, can avoid a lot of ailments of old age ". . . many disorders of old age are a result of avoidable lifestyle factors such as excessive drinking, smoking, bad eating habits and insufficient activity" (Dooghe, 1992: 48). Grimley Evans *et al.*, in a recent report for the Carnegie Trust, similarly observe that "older people have considerable scope for improving their own health by choice of lifestyle," but note that, to do this, they need to be accurately informed and offered appropriate opportunities (Grimley Evans *et al.*, 1992: 77).

Increasing attention is being paid world wide to the potential for health promotion among older people (Grundy and Harrop, 1992a) even if this is still poorly developed in the primary care services of nearly all European countries. People now in their forties, it could be argued, are more likely to be receptive to "healthy living" messages than their parents, so that by the time they reach old age, they may have a different health - and hence dependency - profile. Over the next twenty years however, it seems unlikely that there will be dramatic lifestyle changes, at least not sufficient to bring about major differences in health profiles. The full effects of such changes are likely to take somewhat longer.

The Challenge of Dementia

It appears that the number of old people affected by mental deterioration is increasing because of the drop in mortality among the older elderly: "In years gone by, death would have intervened before illness of this kind became apparent" (Jani-Le Bris, 1993a: 25). As yet, there are no pharmacological treatments for the various forms of dementia and progress in the search for a cure in this field is slow (ibid). Research in the US, Great Britain and Scandinavia shows that most of the care of elderly people with dementia is undertaken by families (Rabins, 1985) and dementia represents perhaps the greatest source of stress for informal carers (Jani-Le Bris, 1993a; OECD, 1990a). Extreme behavioural problems can lead to the "breaking point" at which carers feel they can no longer continue to support their elderly relatives.

Very few reliable data on dementia are available for the European Union as a whole. We do know that the incidence of dementia increases with age; it has been estimated, for instance, that 20% of people aged 80 or more suffer some form of dementing illness (Askham and Thompson, 1990). However these estimates may be regarded as somewhat tentative and problems in making specific diagnoses make it difficult to estimate the likely future incidence, even assuming that there will be no significant medical breakthroughs in the next twenty years. An attempt was made in a study cited in the Danish report to the European Foundation to establish the likely future prevalence of dementia. Although the basis for classification is not clear this study estimated that between 30,000 and 40,000 Danes are senile to a socially disabling degree and suggested that ". . . as the number of elderly increases, the number with senile dementia (in Denmark) is expected to increase to 50,000-70,000 within the next 20 years, if no new treatments are discovered" (cited in Schou et al, 1993). Clearly, this would represent not only an increase in the number of elderly people requiring assistance but a considerable shift in the type and intensity of care required.

Routes to Independence? Housing and Technology

The type, quality and location of elderly people's housing can have a significant impact upon their capacity for independent living. Accommodation occupied by elderly people varies not only within Member States but also between them. Partly because they are likely to have occupied their homes for longer than younger people, elderly people are especially likely to live in homes which are difficult and expensive to maintain and in some countries (e.g. Spain) there are tax disincentives to moving to a new, more convenient and less expensive home. Future demand for care could depend to a considerable extent on the housing policies of the various Member States and the level of provision of purpose built or specially adapted housing for elderly people with disabilities. One positive factor is the almost inevitable improvement which will occur (albeit slowly) in overall housing standards in Member States and the current range of innovative schemes being developed in different European Union countries.

Another related factor which has the potential to make it easier for elderly people to remain living in their own homes might be termed "assistive technology". Many of the problems with which elderly people require assistance relate to their ability to manipulate objects (as in dressing, cooking, etc.) and move about the house. A recent report has observed that "Regarding activity of daily living (ADL) needs, technological innovations offer enormous potential to increase the independence of the elderly, improve their quality of life and *reduce the burden of care now being carried by others.*" (Work Research Centre/EKOS, 1991: 92) (emphasis added).

The same report observes that awareness of the availability of such innovations is low and that "there is already evidence that many useful innovations in assistive devices are not being used by elderly people who could benefit from them" (op cit: 5). Among devices currently available, home security/alert alarms, telephone links, low vision aids, low hearing aids, manipulative devices, and mobility aids all have the potential to increase elderly people's independence. (For useful discussions see: Work Research Centre/EKOS, 1991; Yoxen, 1992). Among the reasons for low use of assistive technology, expense undoubtedly represents a major disincentive for costly items of equipment. There are, however, many inexpensive, easily obtainable items which, if they are marketed appropriately in the future, could have an effect on the demand for care among elderly people. Research at the Age Concern Institute of Gerontology has suggested that elderly people may be unwilling to consider the use of "high tech" home control systems, but it seems likely that the elderly people of the future will be comparatively at home with such technology (Salvage, 1993).

What Do Elderly People Want? Attitudes, Preferences and Choices

The discussion so far has focused on the relatively "hard" factors on the demand side - the increasing numbers of elderly people in the population of the European Union, and likely effects of changes in health care and technology. These factors can be seen in the context of more or less objective "need" for care. To assess the future demand for family care, however, it is also important to look at factors which are likely to affect elderly people's wishes, desires and attitudes towards family care. These preferences will have an interacting and moderating effect on the coming demographic changes and can be aligned more with the common sense notion of "demand". Obviously what elderly people get in terms of family or state care affects - and is affected by - popular and governmental notions of what families "should" provide and to what extent they should be responsible for caring for elderly relatives. Clearly, there is a complex interaction between intergenerational traditions/ behaviour, expectations, political ideology and level of formal provision.

The reports on family care from the eleven European Union Member States brought into sharp focus the great diversity between countries in terms of traditions and ideologies of family care. In Denmark it has been primarily the public sector that cares for elderly people. "During the 1960s and 1970s, concurrently with the entry of women into public life including politics and the labour market, there was an expansion of the welfare state. Public authorities took over many of the obligations formerly borne by the family. At the same time, there was a gradual change in social behaviour. It became increasingly accepted, and was in practice ultimately considered the only correct solution; in educational and human terms, to allow the authorities to take over care of the elderly, children, the sick, etc., by expanding, developing and improving services." (Schou *et al.*, 1993: 62). In the United Kingdom, families have no legal obligation to care for their elderly relatives, but community care policies aimed at enabling people to continue living in their own homes assume high levels of family input and explicitly refer to family care as the cornerstone of community care. In Belgium, parents have a "maintenance obligation" to their children, spouses to one another and children to their parents. "The result of this is that the public welfare centres, which give financial or material support to the needy . . . . must seek to recover these amounts from those responsible for maintenance" (Hedebouw, 1993). In Germany, both taking on the care of elderly relatives and maintaining it under difficult conditions "are largely determined by the attitude that this is taken for granted and that it is a family commitment and obligation" (Döhner *et al.,* 1993).

The Southern European countries may be seen as representing the opposite end of the "family care tradition" spectrum from Denmark. Dontas *et al.* have observed that "the values of Greek society contrast markedly with those of the Anglo-Saxon cultures, for example the notions of personal responsibility for society together with individual independence have little resonance, while that of family responsibility, e.g. for health care, is assumed and constitutes a core value" (Dontas *et al.*, 1990). In Greece, care of elderly relatives is seen as an extension of normal family roles (Triantafillou and Mestheneos, 1993).

In rural Spain, elderly people have a great deal of power in establishing relationships between themselves and their carers: "It is they who decide who is going to care for them. Inheritance and, in the case of daughters, tradition are the essential foundation of this power" (Rodriguez, 1993: 24). Even in urban areas of Spain it is assumed that younger (single or widowed) daughters will care for their parents. "As daughters, they are by definition required to take responsibility for caring for ageing parents: *that is what they are brought up to do, in both the urban and rural environment*" (op cit: 25) (emphasis added).

With this wide diversity of cultural tradition across Europe, it is clear that the expectations of elderly people will differ considerably. We cannot assume that traditions of care will continue in the future, but must, in looking ahead to the next twenty years, bear in mind that future expectations of care in the different member states will vary according to the historical role of the family in caring for elderly people.

Clearly, the preferences elderly people express in terms of source of care are inextricably linked not only with cultural traditions but also with existing social policies and levels of service provision. For Europe as a whole there is a lack of good data on preferences for care, and where research has been undertaken it has generally failed to set stated preferences in the existing cultural/ideological context. It has been suggested that, while elderly people in Southern Europe appear to prefer family care, Northern European elderly people are more likely to favour formal service provision (OECD, 1992). While there may be some truth in this, there are dangers in simplifying matters to this extent; such generalisations are based on very limited data and a wide variety of research methods (Sundstrom, in press). Observed differences may well relate directly to service availability.

Research on preferences for care has often sought specifically to determine elderly people's attitudes to institutional care as opposed to care in their own homes, and most have found prevailing negative views of, and antipathy towards, institutions (Mengani and Gagliardi, 1993; Finch, 1993; Rodriguez, 1993; Walker et al, 1993). Summarising the evidence from the European Foundation national reports, Jani-Le Bris notes a "hostility to residential care which is ubiquitous in Europe" (Jani-Le Bris, 1993: 43). This is not, of course, to suggest that institutional care has no place in Europe. As Glendinning and McLaughlin point out, there will always be some individuals whose care needs are such that institutional care is preferable and desirable (Glendinning and McLaughlin, 1993). If residential care were to be made significantly more attractive to potential residents, the pattern of demand could change considerably.

Those studies which have addressed the issue (and there would appear to have been relatively few of these, mainly in Northern Europe) suggest that elderly people do not, in general, wish to live with their families (Doty, 1986; Waerness, 1989; Jamieson, 1990; Sundstrom, in press). Instead it seems they would prefer what has been termed "intimacy at a distance"; that is "they want to be on good terms with (their children), but they do not want to rely on them too directly" (Finch, 1989: 29). Where services have been made readily available, research suggests that these come to be absorbed into cultural tradition to the extent that they are seen as a "right" (Daatland, 1990; Jani-Le Bris, 1993a). Thus, in those European Union countries with well-established provision, future demand for services is likely to be stronger than in those with less well-developed services.

Evidence from Northern Europe suggests that, even where there are expectations that the family will provide care, there are limits to what people expect their family to provide (Salvage, 1985; Finch and Mason, 1990). Research here also suggests that there is generally a clear "hierarchy" of preferred carers. In the UK, the spouse (where an individual is married) is the first choice followed by any relative living in the household, a daughter, daughter in law, son and finally another relative (Qureshi, 1986). In the national reports for Belgium, Greece and the UK, the preferred hierarchy of care was: spouse, daughter, daughter-in-law, son, other blood relative, other (Finch *et al.*, 1993; Hedebouw, 1993; Triantafillou and Mestheneos, 1993). Finch and Mason (1990a) found that, in Britain a daughter was the overwhelming choice among (all age) respondents for assistance to an elderly woman living alone and requiring assistance with getting up and going to bed. Preferences for care do not occur in a vacuum. They depend not only on cultural traditions, but also on available options (and, of course, awareness of - and feasibility of using - those options).

How will Preferences Change?

When it comes to decision-making about care provision, European studies "suggest very strongly that the older people themselves have the least influence in the decision making process". Their relatives "have, at times, some influence, although this is variable and seems less so in Denmark. Everywhere decisions are dominated by the professionals in the system . . ." (Jamieson, 1991: 263).

In most European Union countries, real choice of care does not exist. The public supply of home care services and residential accommodation is very poorly developed in the four Southern Member States and "even in the more northerly states which have been spending considerable resources for a number of decades on their geriatric/social policies, a situation of genuine choice is rarely guaranteed, except perhaps in Denmark" (Jani-Le Bris, 1993a: 62). Walker observes that ". . . most older people in need of care (in Europe) have very little choice, if any at all, about the service they receive (both in terms of the type of service and its intensity)" (Walker, 1992: 20).

Clearly, an all important question in terms of future demand for family care is that of how, if at all, attitudes and preferences for care are likely to change in the future. Several studies have suggested that attitudes towards accepting formal care services become more positive as higher levels of service provision are introduced (Midré and Synak, 1989; Daatland, 1990) and the authors of the Greek Report for the European Foundation observed that the younger generations in Greece were becoming "more like the modern families of Northern Europe" (Triantafillou and Mestheneos, 1993: 21). In Spain, it has been found that present-day carers "doubted that their own children would look after them and were afraid they would end up in an old people's home" (Rodriguez, 1993: 40). Those who have grown up familiar with the provisions of the Welfare State will undoubtedly have higher expectations of state care than some of today's elderly people. In their awareness of alternatives, it may be that many elderly people of the future will reflect on the care they gave their own parents and elect not to make demands on their own children. Table 5 (taken from the recent Eurobarometer Survey) found that a high proportion of elderly people in all European Union countries feel that "families are less willing to care for older relatives than they used to be".

Expectations are changing. What elderly people want and expect in the future in terms of family care may well be very different from what they expect today and even where family traditions are particularly strong - as in Southern Europe - expectations will continue to change. With the rise of feminism throughout the European Union, women coming into old age will be less likely to accept the 'status quo' and more vociferous in their demands for choice of care.

Political/Economic Factors

Two further factors which have the potential to affect elderly people's demand for care in the future are their purchasing power (in terms of their resources to purchase care) and their political power.

Table 5 : Families are less willing to care for older relatives than they used to be (older people only)

	EC12	Belgium	Denmark	France	West Germany	East Germany	All Germany	Greece	Ireland	Italy	Luxembourg	Netherlands	Portugal	Spain	UK
Agree strongly	33.4	32.4	32.7	41.4	24.3	22.8	24.0	36.0	25.6	39.4	39.2	34.4	42.9	45.2	26.4
Agree slightly	34.0	37.2	26.6	32.7	39.0	30.2	37.2	35.5	26.6	34.6	24.1	27.8	36.2	34.8	31.8
Disagree slightly	18.2	17.7	19.4	13.7	23.8	28.7	24.8	15.1	19.0	17.1	17.4	19.1	12.6	10.5	18.9
Disagree strongly	10.4	9.2	16.4	9.5	8.9	15.4	10.2	7.8	22.5	5.1	11.9	12.5	4.9	5.5	18.3
OK	4.1	3.6	4.8	2.6	4.0	2.9	3.7	5.4	6.3	3.8	7.5	6.2	3.5	4.1	5.3

Source: Walker (1993:29)

Elderly People's Incomes

In all industrial societies, retirement income is built on four "pillars": a basic pension provided by the state together with other social security income; a supplementary occupational pension; personal savings and employment income (Reday-Mulvey, 1990). The 1993 report of the European Observatory notes that: "It is the rights of access to these different sources of income and, of course, the levels at which they are provided that determine the economic security of older people. Thus economic security in old age is primarily a function of the interaction of socio-economic status during working life and the pension system that has developed in a particular country" (Walker et al., 1993: 20). Among European Union countries employment income plays a relatively small part (although there are considerable variations); with state pensions providing the bulk of income (ibid).

National reports indicate that, in the majority of countries, the living standards of elderly people have risen in recent years, along with those of the population as a whole (Walker et al., 1993: 26), suggesting that economic and social policies have had some success in raising the incomes of elderly people. On closer scrutiny however, this progressive development "is seen to derive from different factors in different countries and to be uneven in its impact on the older population" (op cit: 26-27), so that it is not possible to state unequivocally that the economic and social policies of all Member States have specifically targeted elderly people or that policies to improve their living standards have been universally beneficial. Despite some examples of pro-active policy intervention, "it is still a minority of governments that have taken such action. In the majority of cases rising living standards appear to be primarily a 'passive' by-product of increases in the scope and coverage of occupational pensions as a result of collective bargaining and pension scheme maturation . . . ." (Walker et al., 1993: 28-29).

A recent Eurostat analysis revealed wide variations between Member States in the extent of poverty among elderly people, and some slight improvement in the early 1980s (Eurostat, 1990). Despite this improvement, however, the poverty rate among the over-65s in the majority of countries remained above the average rate for that country's population. The 1993 European Observatory report similarly noted "a continuing problem of poverty among a minority of older people, with the size of the minority varying considerably between countries" (Walker et al., 1993: 32) (Table 6).

Table 6 : Poverty among older people in the EC[a]. Poverty index (national poverty rate = 100)

	1980	1985	1985 (000s)	Variation in the absolute number of the poor %
Belgium	175	181	144	-17.7
Denmark	238	255	157	+12.1
France	159	136	1,513	-31.2
Germany (FDR)	136	141	1,263	-8.1
Greece	145	153	371	-2.9
Ireland	163	76	54	-50.5
Italy	132	129	1,447	+1.5
Netherlands	44	46	91	+31.9
Portugal	139	139	545	+8.1
Spain	157	125	1,080	-2.9
UK	163	119	1,846	-7.1

Note[a] Poverty defined as below 50 per cent of National Average Equivalent Expenditure. Older people are those aged 65 and over.

Source: Eurostat, 1990 (in Grundy & Harrop, 1992a:177)

In particular, the Observatory report noted the persistence and widening of income inequalities among older people. Two sources of inequality were identified: age and gender. Younger pensioners, with access to newer forms of private pension, appear to be comparatively better off than older pensioners mainly reliant on non-contributory old age pensions, social assistance and their families. Growing inequalities also exist between older men and women. Women are more likely than men to survive into advanced old age, and to have higher needs for care, and among younger pensioners, women are likely to have poorer retirement incomes than men. In Germany the average retirement pension paid to women in 1990 was just 42% of the male average; in 1989 women formed 76% of social assistance recipients aged 60 and over and 83% of those aged 75 and over (Walker *et al.*, 1993: 46).

Unless the issue of gender inequalities is addressed, poverty among elderly women is likely to persist. With all the European Union countries facing an increasing number of elderly people in their populations and lower numbers of younger working people, retrenchment in welfare spending are likely, and it may well be that, in the future, private pensions will become more important as a source of income in old age. There is evidence of a 'polarisation' of the elderly populations of some European Union countries, with the wealthiest becoming wealthier and the poorest failing to maintain their share in rising prosperity (see Kelly, 1994). If this trend continues, very elderly women, and especially those without private or occupational pensions, will be especially likely to have to rely heavily on unpaid family care.

Trends in Retirement and Pensions

Potential income in old age depends partly on the statutory age of retirement, which covers a broad range across European Union Member States from 55 for women in Italy to 67 (men and women) in Denmark (Commission of the European Communities 1992a) (Table 7).

Table 7: General statutory pensionable age for employees, 1991

	Males	Females
Belgium	60	60
Denmark	67	67
France	60	60
Germany	65	65
Greece	65	60
Ireland	65	65
Italy	60	55
Luxembourg	65	65
Netherlands	65	65
Portugal	65	62
Spain	65	65
UK	65	60

Source: Commission of the European Communities, 1993a:26

Over the last twenty years there has been an accelerating trend towards early labour force exit among older workers; in several Member States this has been encouraged by public policy in response to rising unemployment (Walker *et al.*, 1993). The 1993 European Observatory report suggested, however, that the encouragement of early exit from the labour force has failed to have a dramatic effect on the employment situation of younger people, and Jani-Le Bris notes that use of "early exit" arrangements among Member States occurred, "paradoxically" at a time when demographic changes have led to large increases in the number of elderly people and the "concomitant need to provide care for dependency" (Jani-Le Bris, 1993a: 119).

There have been substantial changes in the employment rate in the over-55 age group over the last 20 years. According to the OECD the employment rate in this age group fell by an average of 12.5 points between 1965 and 1990 (cited in Commission of the European Communities, 1992a: 36). Since the 'working population' also includes job-seekers, however, and given that unemployment is particularly high in this age group anyway, "it is clear that the variations in the (active) employment rate are actually much more spectacular." (Commission of the European Communities, 1992a: 36).

Recent policy innovations across Europe will serve to emphasise the 'retirement - pension' gap; that is the length of time between average age of actual retirement and age at which the statutory pension becomes payable. In the job market, older people typically encounter retention and discharge problems by the time they reach the age of 55 (Commission of the European Communities, 1993b). Yet in many of the European Union States today, attempts are being made (due partly to awareness of demographic changes which will mean that fewer younger workers will be available to generate the income that supports social spending and partly to awareness of the welfare spending pressures caused by an ageing population) to *increase* the statutory age of retirement (Commission of the European Communities, 1992a). In the context of the debate which is taking place in most EU countries on the financing of long-term care for dependent elderly people and social security in general (including pensions) (Pacolet *et al.*, 1993), there is a trend towards equalisation of pension ages for men and women, and tightening of the conditions for receipt of pensions. The motivation of workers (especially those without private or occupational pension provision) to continue working to older ages is therefore likely to increase.

Political Power

Spending power is to some extent dependent on political power - the ability of elderly people to make their needs and wishes known and to ensure that these needs and wishes are met. Political power also influences the use of public funds - both for pensions and for service development. At present, levels of engagement of elderly people in political or pressure group activities are very low (Walker, 1993). A report from the Netherlands observes that "Notably lacking in many countries is a conscious and sophisticated effort on the part of the elderly to organise themselves as a viable and potent political force." (Institute for Bioethics/Hastings Center, 1993: 10). In the few countries where elderly people have organised themselves politically "the benefits have been striking: the elderly become a political power to be reckoned with, a point not lost on legislators" (ibid).

Developments *are* occurring, however, at both national and European levels. In March 1992 a meeting of a European Seniors Parliament took place in Luxembourg over two days, which included 518 older people from all twelve Member States. The aim of the parliament was to discuss issues related to ageing at a European Union level, and one of the results was that a European Senior Citizens' Charter (previously drawn up) was discussed and voted through, the aim of which was to represent the interests of older people across the European Union. The Charter stresses, among other things, the rights of elderly people to autonomy, security, and dignity in terms of income, housing, residential, health and community services and to responsible participation in decision-making through effective participation on administrative bodies. (Crosby, 1993). In 1993, the European Year of Older People and Solidarity Between Generations focused attention on the need to promote international co-operation and exchanges between organisations representing older people (Commission of the European Communities, 1993b). Such exchanges could facilitate and strengthen elderly people's political action across the European Union.

By 2015, not only will elderly people represent a higher proportion of the voting population of the European Union than they do today; there is every likelihood that they will be more educated, more articulate, more prepared to demand services which they see as a "right" and more willing and able to organise themselves politically. 'Pensioner power' is now recognised as a force to be reckoned with in the Netherlands, where two fledgling political parties representing the nation's elderly people took seven of the 150 parliamentary seats in the recent general election (The Guardian, 1994). Wilson has drawn attention to a widespread belief that elderly people of the future "will be less passive, have higher expectations and be more demanding than current pensioners" (Wilson, 1993: 93). The role of male carers, Wilson reminds us, must not be forgotten here. Caregiving husbands, she suggests, "may join politically with the great majority of older women who are caregivers and receivers to force some changes in formal caring (op cit: 102). In short, we cannot assume that elderly people will accept the existing pattern of care provision from family, state, private, voluntary and other sources.

Summary: The Potential Demand for Family Care of Elderly People

1. Population projections suggest that, by the year 2015, there are likely to be an extra 14 million people aged 60 or more in the population of the European Union, including an extra 4 million aged 80 and over. A quarter of the European Union population would then be aged 60 or over.

2. At present the majority of elderly people remain able to live independently. What proportion will be able to do so in twenty years' time depends on many factors, including preventive health care, developments in technology and housing conditions. In the absence of research developments, the incidence of dementia is likely to increase substantially with significant implications for care, including higher levels of emotional and psychological stress for informal carers and increasing demands on carers' time.

3. Traditions of family care vary widely across the Member States of the European Union but in most, elderly people do not currently have 'real' choice of sources of assistance. Despite emphases by State policies on 'care in the community' (which assume continuance of family care) most elderly people in countries where research has been undertaken express a preference for only limited reliance on their families.

4. Despite improvements, poverty among elderly people remains high in the European Union, and there is a general trend towards rethinking welfare systems. With increasing use of occupational and private pensions in some countries, however, living standards are likely to improve for some elderly people over the next twenty years, but there is likely to be a continuing polarisation of the elderly population into those with occupational or private pensions and those without.

5. At present, elderly people's political power is very limited. With elderly people representing an increasing proportion of the voting populations of the Member States, increasing levels of education and increasing acceptance of the need to take service users' views into account, it is likely that elderly people in the future will be more vociferous in expressing their wishes. The demands of the elderly people of the future (who will have had different life-experiences and different attitudes and expectations) may be for provisions which will enable them to live independently of family support.

CHAPTER 3: THE POTENTIAL SUPPLY OF FAMILY CARE FOR OLDER PEOPLE

Family Care: Alive and Well

The general importance of the family and other informal networks in providing support and care is now widely acknowledged (Jamieson, 1991); the contribution made by these networks is clear when we note that at least eight out of ten of those with care needs in Europe live in private households (Glendinning and McLaughlin, 1993: 9). Even in Denmark, where service provision is comparatively widespread, and where the state assumes more responsibility than elsewhere in Europe, the family still plays a significant part in supporting elderly relatives (Schou *et al.*, 1993; Jamieson, 1991). While there is an increasing tendency for elderly people to live alone, close ties are maintained with families - according to a recent survey, nearly four out of five elderly people in Europe see a member of their family at least once a week on average, with nearly half seeing a family member daily (Walker, 1993).

Where services are provided, there appears to be little evidence that they 'drive out' informal care; drawing on evidence from Danish, Dutch and French contributors, Jamieson concludes that the evidence generally suggests that services *"complement rather than substitute"* for informal care (Jamieson, 1991: 258) (author's emphasis).

That the family remains the predominant provider of help to elderly people in Europe is demonstrated by numerous studies (see for example, Jamieson, 1991; Jani-Le Bris, 1993a; Infratest, 1993; Stevenson, 1993). Johnson has recently observed the "remarkable persistence of family support and the very high level of personal responsibility accepted for family members" (Johnson, 1993: 19), while Finch and Mason have drawn attention to the fact that family care of elderly people is treated as essentially *unremarkable;* that is, in effect, taken for granted by both sides (Finch and Mason, 1992). Despite increases in many countries in state service provision, the family remains by far the greatest provider of help for elderly people. At issue here, however, is the question of whether this situation is likely to be sustained in the future.

Influences on the Future Supply of Care

Throughout the European Union, care of elderly people is predominantly family care. To what extent is this resource likely to remain over the next twenty years? Clearly, there are many factors to be taken into account here (see Figure 1). In terms of families themselves, it seemed appropriate to look separately at questions of ability/opportunity (to what extent will family members in the future be *able* to provide care for older relatives?) and at those of willingness/motivation (how *willing* will family members be to provide care?). In terms of ability to care, it will obviously be necessary to consider changes in dependency ratios - in particular the numbers of potential carers who will be available in the future - and evidence from research on attitudes to giving care to older relatives. Divorce and remarriage are on the increase in Europe, so the implications of these will obviously have to be considered. Fertility rates, age of child-bearing and possible overlaps between the care of children and of elderly people will all have to be taken into account, as will likely future patterns of migration.

Existing financial and service support is likely to affect not only ability to care, but also *willingness* to care, and the health status of future potential carers will also be considered. Of particular importance in terms of carer availability may be future levels of family employment - particularly that of women in their middle years who (in the UK) represent approximately half of all family carers.

Looking at the extent to which families will be *willing* to provide care in the future, it will obviously be important to look at what motivates family members to give care, and at what factors lead them to want to stop caring. It will be necessary to assess the evidence as to the level of conflict between work outside the home and caring inside the home, and look at the kinds of support carers say they need to continue caring.

Future patterns of family care will be related to the availability of alternative sources of care, which will vary according to current service provision. These, in turn, depend upon state policies and ideologies about what role the family should play in the care of elderly people and the respective roles of the private (market) and voluntary sectors.

Finally, account must be taken of economic factors which are likely to affect future patterns of care for elderly people. Economic growth or recession, competing financial demands (e.g. for health care or unemployment support) and shifts in financial allocation priorities will clearly have the potential to alter what families are required to do for their elderly relatives.

Caring in the 90s: Who are the Carers?

Before discussing the future potential for family care in the European Union, it is important to establish a clear profile of today's carers. Due to the absence of surveys based on representative national samples in most Member States, information on the characteristics of carers is incomplete. "The information which exists normally derives from small samples of an unrepresentative kind, linked moreover to one town or one region; certain pieces of information exclude spouses as carers, while others draw no distinction on the basis of relationship to the dependent person . . ." (Jani-Le Bris, 1993a: 52). Most informal carers are women; Waerness observes that "the expectations of care and service and the responsibility for the physical and emotional well-being of the family members, are laid mainly on the female members of the family (Waerness, 1989: 217). However, the contribution of men to the care of elderly people (mainly as spouses) is very considerable and generally unacknowledged. Estimates of the number of carers who are spouses (and therefore likely to be elderly themselves) vary somewhat. The recent Eurobarometer survey (Walker, 1993), looking at the European Union as a whole found that adult children were the most frequently mentioned main carers (40%) followed by spouses (32%), other relatives (14%), public social services (13%), private paid help (11%), friends (6%), neighbours (6%) and voluntary organisations (3%) (Walker, 1993). Elsewhere it is suggested that the main group of carers is spouses, among whom there are as many men as women in some countries (Britain, Ireland and the Netherlands and probably other countries in the centre and north of the community) (Jani-Le Bris, 1993a). Among descendants, females certainly predominate in all Member States: "daughters and, generally to a smaller proportion, daughters-in-law, form a large majority of this group" (Jani-Le Bris, 1993a: 53).

In terms of the proportions of carers in different age groups, little information is available on a Europe-wide basis. Some of the national reports (see Appendix 1) were able to supply information on the age of carers, but "taken together they are insufficient to allow valid deductions to be made as regards the possible influence of this variable, closely linked to the health and hence to the capacity to provide care, especially over the long term" (Jani-Le Bris, 1993a: 55).

In the UK, nearly half (46%) of all carers were aged between 50 and 74 in 1985, and one-fifth of people in this age group defined themselves as carers (Askham *et al.*, 1992). Children who provide care for elderly parents do so with little support not only from formal services, but also from other family members (Kendig, 1986); a fact which was highlighted in a number of the national reports to the European Foundation. In Belgium, it is reported that over half the carers (54%) do all the work alone, with 23% having help from a second carer, 17% having two helpers and 6% having three (Hedebouw, 1993). In Spain, "the family appoints one person as carer and virtually abandons her to her task" (Rodriguez, 1993: 29), while in the UK a report on a national survey published in 1988 revealed that half of all carers said that no-one helped them with their caring tasks (Green, 1988). Unless steps are taken to reverse this pattern, it seems likely that the tendency for 'principal carers' to be "left to care alone" (Wright, 1986) will continue in the future, with a strong likelihood that an increasing incidence of dementia among elderly people will begin to make significantly increased demands on a smaller 'pool' of available carers, many of whom have their own health problems.

Carers: Ability to provide care

Many future carers, of course, will be spouses - a fact which in itself will have significant implications for policy as most will be elderly themselves. The potential availability of children to care for elderly parents in the future will depend to an important extent on:

(a) Fertility rates (that is, the number of children born per woman)
(b) Remarriage and divorce rates.

The first of these, the effects of which are much the more clear cut of the two, will be discussed first.

Changes in Fertility Rates

The drop in fertility which has been a feature of the European Union as a whole has significant implications for the future care of elderly people. As already observed, apart from care provided by spouses, most of the family care provided for elderly people comes from daughters or daughters-in-law. The lower the number of children born, the lower the potential 'caretaker pool' becomes; between 1960 and 1991 the total fertility rate (average number of children per woman) fell from 2.61 to 1.51 (Eurostat, 1993a: Table E-1).

Walker *et al.* (1993), taking as a "crude indicator" of the care taker potential within the family system the ratio of women aged 45 to 69 to people aged over 69, demonstrate the extent to which this potential shrank in European Union countries between 1960 and 1990 (Table 8). As people who gave birth during the baby boom years come into old age towards the end of this century, there will actually be an *increase* in the number of children potentially able to offer care, but by 2015, it will be the baby boom generation themselves who are coming into old age and the number of children available to care for them will be considerably reduced. Applying Eurostat population projections for the year 2015, it would appear that the caregiver ratio for the European Union as a whole could be in the region of

1.3 (that is 1.3 women in the 45 to 69 age group for every one person aged 70 and over) (based on Eurostat, 1991: Table I-5). As we move beyond the temporary baby boom peak, the effects of falling fertility rates will really begin to be seen.

Table 8: The shrinkage of the female care taker potential in EC countries, 1960-1990 (women aged 45-69 in proportion to population 70+)

	1990	1960	Reduction %
Belgium	1.42	2.00	71
Denmark	(1.97)[1]	-	-
France	1.33	-	-
Germany	1.57	2.64	59
Greece	1.70	-	-
Ireland	1.40	1.60	87
Italy	1.60	2.30	70
Luxembourg	1.61	2.43	66
Netherlands	1.48	2.16	69
Portugal	1.60	2.50	64
Spain	1.53	2.48	62
UK	1.28	-	-
Mean (11 countries)	1.50	-	-
(8 countries)	1.53	2.26	68.5

[1] Women aged 45-64 in proportion to population 65+

Source: Walker et al, 1993:104

Remarriage and Divorce

The rate of divorce is increasing in the countries of the European Union. Although most commentators agree that it is difficult to predict precisely what effect this will have on family care in the future (Finch, 1989: 111,113; Stevenson, 1993), most appear to be in agreement that it at least has the potential to blur the lines of responsibility for the care of older relatives.

The increase in divorce may be attributed to a number of different factors (Boh, 1989). Between 1968 and 1974, the law concerning divorce which had previously been very restrictive, was changed in many countries (Dooghe, 1992). "In most countries the conditions and the procedures to divorce were

Table 9 : Number of marriages and divorces in the countries of the European Communities

	Marriages			Divorces		
	1965	1988	1965 = index 100	1965	1988	1965 = index 100
Belgium	66,535	59,075	89	5,520	20,809	377
Denmark	41,693	32,080	77	6,527	14,717	225
France	346,308	271,124	78	34,900	106,096	304
Germany (FDR)	492,128	397,738	81	58,728	128,729	219
Greece	80,728	47,873	59	3,505	8,556	244
Ireland	16,946	*17,936	106	-	-	-
Italy	399,009	*315,447	79	-	*30,778	
Luxembourg	2,184	2,079	95	146	780	534
Netherlands	108,517	87,843	81	6,206	27,870	449
Portugal	75,483	71,098	94	695	9,022	1,298
Spain	227,460	*214,898	94	-	*21,126	-
UK	422,100	394,500	93	40,600	165,700	408
European Community	2,279,091	1,911,691	84	156,827	534,200	341

* provisional data

Source: Eurostat, 1990 (in Dooghe, 1992:4)

liberalised, resulting in a strong increase of the number of divorces. In 1965, there were 5,520 divorces in Belgium, twenty years later (1988) already 20, 209." (Dooghe, 1992: 3). Table 9 shows how the number of divorces increased in the countries of the European Union between 1965 and 1988.

Another factor which has undoubtedly affected the rate of divorce has been what Boh refers to as the "individualisation and privatisation" of marriage: "Divorces are seen as a sign of rising personal expectations, a greater orientation towards personal happiness, self-realisation, and a move away from traditional values such as conformity and duty" (Boh, 1989: 281). For the European Union as a whole, the number of divorces per thousand population increased dramatically from 149.8 in 1960 to 580.3 in 1989 (Eurostat, 1993a: Table F-1).

Future rates of divorce in Europe will affect the potential for family care of elderly people in two ways. Firstly, in terms of divorce rates among elderly people themselves, it will affect the potential for spouse care. By 2019 it is estimated that around 15% of all over 65s in Great Britain will have been divorced (McGlone, 1992). Noting that fewer divorced women than men remarry, Finch *et al.* in the UK report for the European Foundation, conclude that it is therefore reasonable to predict that fewer women will be cared for by a spouse in old age in the future than is the case for the present generation of elderly people (Finch *et al.*, 1993).

Secondly, in terms of increases in divorce rate among potential carers, these are likely to complicate issues of family loyalties and responsibilities. Walker (1992) has drawn attention to evidence that divorced children give less help to older relatives than those in stable marriages; as well as providing less direct personal care they are less likely to have social contact with their older relatives (Cicirelli, 1983). "Of course," Walker observes "there are obvious material reasons why divorced children may display lower levels of filial obligation than non-divorced ones, including limited financial resources." (Walker, 1992: 14).

Dooghe reinforces this point: "Often, divorced daughters, facing their own economic problems, are unable to assume additional responsibility for their ageing parent(s)." (Dooghe, 1992: 5). Glendinning and McLaughlin suggest that ". . . the impact of divorce and remarriage may, on the one hand, lead to weakened obligations towards older relatives . . . . On the other hand, the increase in divorce and remarriage may increase the pool of younger generation families and 'step families' who might be willing to help" (Glendinning and McLaughlin, 1993: 15).

In some cases, an increasing divorce rate is likely to result in an increase in previously married children returning to the parental home. In Britain, co-residence with parents has been found to be higher among previously married than among currently married people in the 35 to 44 and 45 to 54 age groups (especially men). "This group would include those unable to re-establish a separate household following marital breakdown" (Grundy and Harrop,

1992b: 331). In this case the potential for family care of elderly people could be increased, but if men predominated, this would be limited by established gender role behaviour.

Apart from the increasing rate of divorce, there are other changes in patterns of family formation which are likely to affect potential for family care in the future. The increasing age at which couples first marry, later age of women at the birth of the first child, and in particular, the greater tendency towards co-habitation rather than marriage and the decline in availability of unmarried daughters and sons all have significant implications for family care. For the European Union as a whole, mean age at first marriage increased from 26.7 in 1960 to 27.6 in 1990 for males and from 24.0 to 25.1 for females (Eurostat, 1993a: Tables F-6 & F-7). Concurrently, mean age of women at birth of the first child has been increasing (Eurostat, 1993a: Table E-13).

Tendencies towards early marriage and marriage in general have diminished - not only for reasons of social insecurity but also because a growing number of young people today postpone marriage or do not wish to marry at all, preferring instead alternative "marriage-like" arrangements (Boh, 1989). In the UK, marriage remains popular in the sense that most people will marry at some stage of their life. The authors of the UK report note that the supply of single daughters and sons (the 'traditional' carers of elderly people) is now much more restricted than in the past and will continue to be very limited (Finch *et al.*, 1993).

In the European Union as a whole, the number of marriages per one thousand population decreased from 8.0 in 1960 to 5.7 in 1991, while the number of live births outside marriage per one thousand population increased from 265.97 to 759.87 (Eurostat, 1993a: Tables E-1 and F-1).

Competing Demands? Child Care and Employment

Two factors which are likely to affect future availability of family care for elderly people are the potentially conflicting demands of child care, on the one hand, and employment on the other.

Child care

Although it might appear that, with potential carers of elderly people having fewer children themselves, they might have more time available to help their parents, this effect will be offset both by the fact that there will be fewer kin to help the generation above and by the fact that children are tending to stay at home for longer periods (e.g. due to youth unemployment) (Hoskins, 1993).

Elderly people themselves may be increasingly called upon to care for grandchildren while the middle generation go to work (Grundy and Harrop, 1992a).

Female Employment

Female employment patterns, especially the increasing participation of married women in the labour force, have frequently been cited as a factor which may influence the amount of family support available for elderly people (Doty, 1986; Coleman and Bond, 1990). Doty observed in 1986 that "since most of the family care of impaired elders not provided by spouses has traditionally been provided by middle-aged adult daughters and daughters-in-law, many experts believe that the increasing trend towards women in the labour force is likely to decrease the capacity of these traditional care givers to meet the care needs of impaired elderly relatives" (Doty, 1986: 40). Paukert (1984) has drawn attention to the dramatic increases which have occurred in the labour force participation of women over the last two decades (Paukert, 1984). Employment of women, as Boh points out, does not necessarily depend only on economic factors "but is related to employment policies, which in turn are shaped by prevailing family ideologies, political practices, historical traditions and cultural values and norms" (Boh, 1989: 271).

Activity rates for women vary considerably across the European Union, with Spain, Greece and Italy having comparatively low, and the Northern countries - Denmark, UK, Netherlands and Germany (excluding the new German Lander in the East) having higher rates (Commission for the European Communities, 1992b).

Table 10 shows how the employment rate varied for women aged between 15 and 64 in the Member States in 1990. The lowest female employment rate at that time was in Spain (31% of the female population aged 15 to 64) with the highest (Denmark) having more than twice as many women in employment (72%).

Several writers have recognised the shift from the traditional model of the family with the husband/ father as breadwinner and the wife/mother as a full time housewife to the dual-work family in which both husband and wife are employed outside the home as one of the most significant changes which has occurred in family patterns this century (Boh, 1989; Waerness, 1989; Johnson, 1993). Johnson suggests that, as the involvement of women in the labour force increases their ability to act in the role of unpaid carer may be in question (Johnson, 1993).

Table 10 : Women's employment and unemployment rates, EC, 1990, % of population aged 15- 64

	Employed and unemployed	Employed	Unemployed
Belgium	52	41	11
Denmark	81	72	9
France	63	51	12
Germany	61	55	6
Greece	51	39	12
Ireland	51	36	15
Italy	53	37	16
Luxembourg	44	42	2
Netherlands	58	47	11
Portugal	63	56	7
Spain	55	31	24
UK	70	63	7

Source: Employment in Europe 1992, DG Employment, Industrial Relations and Social Affairs, Office for Official Publications of the European Communities, Luxembourg: pp 36-9 (in Glendinning & McLaughlin, 1993:6)

With fewer young people in the work force, and with increasing divorce rates (which will push many women - temporarily at least - into the need for economic self reliance), it appears likely that there will be a continued need for women to work outside the home in the future. The question of whether women are likely to *wish* to go into paid employment, and the extent to which this desire is likely to conflict with the care needs of old people is discussed below (see 'Carers: Willingness to Provide Care').

Health: Future Prospects for Carers

If the current focus on preventive health care (including attempts to change health behaviour) apparent in some EU countries continues and develops, a gradual improvement in the health of this group is likely. However, it is important to remember that many carers will themselves be elderly and therefore subject to the same health problems as elderly people in general. Many studies have testified to the levels of stress experienced by informal carers as a result of looking after elderly relatives and Evers has observed that "stress perceived" in matters of care is strongly shaped by what is seen as "justified" or normal by carers. The same "objective stress" is felt very differently depending on the self-images of carers and what they perceive as their rights and duties, those of their spouses and likewise as the responsibilities of the Welfare State (Evers, 1992: 8). Thus while "objective" physical health is likely to be directly affected by any increasing demands of family care (and the national reports do suggest that many carers suffer health problems of their own) the extent to which carers perceive their own health to be affected by their caring tasks is likely to depend a great deal on changing norms and values.

Service and Financial Support for Carers

The availability of financial, practical and emotional support for carers will undoubtedly be an important factor in determining the ability of families to provide support for their elderly relatives in the future.

Financial and service provision specifically for carers varies considerably across the European Union. In Denmark, where public sector provision of services is highly developed, there is no specific, practical or financial support for informal carers simply because (notwithstanding the fact that families do provide assistance) care of elderly people is not regarded as a family responsibility (Schou *et al.*, 1993). In Greece, the lack of specific support for carers relates not to highly developed service provision but to the existence of a strong cultural tradition of family responsibility and lack of formal support (Triantafillou and Mestheneos, 1993).

While some Member States do provide some degree of financial support for carers (e.g. United Kingdom, France, Netherlands) such support tends to be more in the nature of a "token" payment than a realistic compensation for hours spent in caring or earnings foregone (For a discussion, see Glendinning & McLaughlin, 1993). In some countries, respite care services have developed partly in recognition of informal carers' need for a break and self-help groups are beginning to emerge, along with national and local carers' organisations. However, provision of services specifically designed to support carers either physically, psychologically or emotionally remain very much the exception rather than the rule; the tradition of providing services geared to elderly people's needs - rather than those of the family as a unit - remains strong. Many services provided for elderly people do, of course, indirectly assist their informal carers, but if families are to be expected to continue to provide high levels of assistance for elderly relatives in the face of declining caregiver ratios and longer periods of dependency, service provision will increasingly have to take their needs and abilities into account.

Migration

By comparison with fertility and mortality, international migration has been a relatively minor element in overall population change over the post war period; countries where migration was relatively important include France and Germany, which registered large inflows in the 1950s and the 1960s, and Ireland and Portugal which experienced substantial outflows. Following the economic downturn from around 1973, international migratory flows were considerably reduced and there was also some reversal of earlier patterns, with a return of migrants from a number of industrialised European countries to some of the less industrialised areas (op cit).

The development of a Europe-wide labour market will lead to increased mobility between countries (DaneAge, N/D; Room, 1991; Naegele and Reichert, 1993; Commission of the European Communities, 1993a). The extent to which migration rates within and from the European Union will lead to the isolation of elderly people is not, at this stage, possible to estimate.

Apart from international migration, migration within individual Member States has had a considerable effect upon patterns of family life. Thus during the 1960s and 1970s, the demographic profile of Greece changed "rapidly and dramatically" due to a large scale immigration of young Greeks to industrialised countries and "to an equally large and continuing internal migration to large urban centres." (Dontas *et al.*, 1990: 3).

Jani-Le Bris observes that the "relative closeness" of national rates of ageing in the European Union countries for the years around 1990 "masks major regional disparities in most countries." "Most of these" she notes, "can be attributed to internal migration: in brief, young people leave the countryside to set themselves up in industrialised areas, or areas that are being industrialised; they marry, have children and contribute to heavy urbanisation of the area. Meanwhile, older people stay in the villages, whose loss of younger population is especially important in rural areas, distant from the zones of development" (Jani-Le Bris, 1993a: 13). Harris (1983) has argued that the tendency for young people to move away from home to establish an independent unit will tend to weaken the bases of parent-child relations. There is, however, evidence to suggest that geographical mobility has less potential effect on intergenerational proximity than is generally assumed; with a high proportion of elderly people living within close proximity of their children (CBGS, 1975, 1985).

Apart from the potential effects of the migration of younger people, enhanced mobility within the European Union is also likely to affect elderly people. Inter-State migration upon retirement will have implications not only for social protection, but also for patterns of family care; but again it is not possible to judge to what extent this is likely to affect elderly people's need for care over the next 20 years. Enhanced mobility within European Union countries may also increase the use, among middle class families, of cheap migrant labour as a replacement for family care.

Future trends in international migration are uncertain (OECD, 1988). However, in comparison with changes in fertility and mortality rates, migration has had and will probably continue to have a comparatively mild effect on the structure of the European population (OECD, 1988).

Carers: Willingness to Provide Care

Having looked at the 'external' constraints which may affect the ability of families to give care to elderly people in the future - the number of 'potential' carers, the competing demands of child care and employment, physical and psychological health, levels of service and financial support and migration - we now turn to the all-important questions of willingness and motivation. How strong are inter-generational relationships? What have studies of attitudes to and expectations of care-giving revealed about carers? Where do carers draw the line? The relationship between care-giving and employment, and the question of whether a desire for employment is likely to pose a real threat to the care of elderly people in the future are considered.

Intergenerational Relationships

Relationships between generations are multi-faceted and cannot be represented by any single measure (see, for example, Hobman *et al.*, 1993). One measure of the extent to which intergenerational solidarity exists, however - described by Walker (1993) as the "acid test" of intergenerational relations - is the extent to which younger people are willing to pay taxes and contributions to fund pensions. In a recent Eurobarometer survey, people aged 15 and over in the Member States of the European Union were asked whether they agreed or disagreed with the statement that those in employment have a duty to ensure, through the contributions on taxes they pay, that older people have a "decent standard of living". A high proportion of people agreed with this statement (in the European Union as a whole, 37% agreed strongly and 43% agreed slightly) suggesting that "the social contract is in good shape" (Walker, 1993: 15).

Attitudes to Giving Care

In terms of the availability of family care, it has been suggested that "cultural and economic factors and changes in the willingness and ability to care, are likely to be much more important than fluctuations in the size of the relevant age cohorts" (Kraan *et al.*, 1991: 228). Attitudes towards caring for elderly relatives are extremely difficult to measure. Feelings concerning what one would do in a hypothetical situation do not necessarily relate closely to what one would actually do were that situation to arise, and once embarked on a caring career, feelings of guilt and obligation may override previously held attitudes.

Studies have suggested that resistance to institutional care is as strong among younger people caring for older relatives as it is among older people themselves (e.g. West *et al.*, 1984) and that commitment to the provision of family care remains high. In the German report to the European Foundation, Döhner *et al.* note that, in Germany "accommodation in a home is, in the main, not considered until the carer fears s/he can no longer perform the care work required" (Döhner *et al.*, 1993: 28). In Spain "the great majority (79%) of carers and their families will not even consider the possibility that the old people they care for should go into a rest home, believing that they are cared for better in the family" (Rodriguez, 1993: 21). In Denmark, even though transfer to a nursing home or similar institution "is seen as a natural state of affairs in the case of the elderly who can no longer look after themselves" (Schou *et al.*, 1993: 22), many relatives do still feel a "strong . . . personal obligation to provide help themselves . . ." (op cit: 65).

The strength of family commitment to caring reveals itself in reluctance to accept outside help from public services. In Germany, Bruder *et al.* have drawn attention to low levels of willingness and ability on the part of carers to mobilise support and assistance from others (Bruder *et al.*, 1981). In the Netherlands, Steenvoorden observes that "carers are not themselves . . . quick to ask others for help. Main carers can put up a surprising amount of resistance to the idea of doing something for their own benefit and releasing themselves from the caring role" (Steenvoorden, 1993: 30). The authors of the German report to the European Foundation suggest that this determination to continue to care unsupported even in very difficult circumstances may be explained by the fact that caring for elderly relatives is "taken for granted" and is seen as a "family commitment and obligation" (enforced by law) (Döhner *et al.*, 1993: 51). Jani-Le Bris, drawing on the national reports to the European Foundation, suggests that this resistance to accepting help probably relates partly to psychological resistance to "the intrusion of strangers, dispossessing (carers) of the exclusive intimacy of the patient, part of the decisions and also part of their power", distrust of professionals and the fear of being dependent on any person (Jani-Le Bris, 1993a: 109-110).

Finch and Mason in their British study of filial obligations and kin support for elderly people, concluded that, at the most general level, most people do give assent to the idea of filial obligations (i.e. that adult children are obligated to their parents) but that this assent "is neither universal nor unconditional" (Finch and Mason, 1990: 154). Their data suggest, for instance, that most people consider "that it should not be necessary, even for a woman, to sacrifice her job to care for an elderly relative" (although, nearly all of those who said that someone should give up employment went on to specify the woman - rather than the man, where a choice exists) (Finch and Mason, 1990b: 352).

Motivations: Why Do Carers Care?

The question of why carers care has been addressed in depth in British work (see Finch, 1989), with full discussions of the notions of "obligation" and "duty". Finch observes that "the assumption that it is natural to feel a sense of obligation to one's kin informs much contemporary social policy." (Finch, 1989: 241).

Certainly, notions of "obligation" and "moral duty" as an underpinning for the provision of care emerged clearly from many of the national reports on caring (see, e.g. Finch *et al.*, 1993; Hedebouw, 1993; Schou *et al.*, 1993) but it is also clear that much of this sense of obligation represents an awareness of reciprocal responsibilities - a repayment for care previously given in the past or benefits (e.g. money, child-care) bestowed in the present.

It is clear from the national reports that it is generally assumed that spouses have an intrinsic motivation "for better or for worse" to provide care for one another (Jani-Le Bris, 1993a). In the case of children's obligations to their parents, 'reciprocity' is a consistent theme in the literature. Care may be provided in exchange for financial assistance (Finch, 1989), in return for services (e.g. caring for grandchildren) or simply in repayment of the care that parents have previously given themselves (Qureshi, 1986).

In her book on family responsibilities, Finch argues that kin relationships are marked out distinctively by a sense of obligation "which in the end is a matter of morality rather than individual feelings or emotions" (Finch, 1989: 241). This "sense of obligation" however "is nothing like its image in political debate, where it appears as a set of ready-made moral rules which all right-thinking people accept and put into practice. It is actually much less reliable than that. It is nurtured and grows over time between some individuals more strongly than between others, and its practical consequences are highly variable. It does have a binding quality, *but that derives from commitments built up between real people over many years, not from an abstract set of moral values*" (Finch, 1989: 242) (emphasis added).

Much of the caring literature focuses on the stresses and problems of caring, so that the positive aspects of giving care are frequently forgotten. These "rewards" emerged clearly from the national reports, with carers referring to the enrichment of relationships between generations, enjoyment at seeing the dependant in a happier condition than they had previously enjoyed, the gratitude of elderly relatives for care provided, the endowment of life with "meaning" and the satisfaction of being useful or indispensable to someone (Jani-Le Bris, 1993: 113-4).

In some countries, the rewards of caring are much more material than this and are woven into the very fabric of the intergenerational relationship. In Greece, economic transfers between the generations which occur on marriage - rather than at death - set up very specific obligations as far as the care of elderly relatives is concerned.

There is little evidence from carers themselves of a desire to divest themselves of responsibility, but the extent to which this assumption of responsibility is "a manifestation of internalised oppression" is, as Stevenson suggests, a matter of opinion (Stevenson 1993: 79). The idea, strongly mooted by the governments of many Member States, that more help must come from the family, neighbours and friends, has been strongly criticised by the women's movement on the grounds that such responsibility would mostly land on the shoulders of women (Steenvoorden, 1993).

During the 1970s and 1980s, feminist academics developed theoretical analyses of the family and the welfare state (Morris, 1991). The interrelationship between the two was particularly apparent in the boom in research and theorising on the issue of 'carers'. "Feminists exposed the way that the state exploits women's unpaid labour within the home and the extent to which the policies of caring for elderly and disabled people within the community depend upon women's role within the family." (op cit: 146). Even if state provision expanded so that adequate care was provided by paid carers, it has been argued, the family would still remain the setting for community care, and as the family is the setting of women's oppression, the fundamental dependence of women would remain unquestioned (Finch, 1984). In Britain, the rise of the feminist critique coincided with the development of carers' pressure groups and with an increasing focus in public policy on the needs of informal carers.

As yet the feminist critique of community care (which questions the notions of "obligation" and "duty") does not appear to have undermined family care in any of the Member States. While there are certainly moves in some countries towards a new awareness of carers' rights, commitment to caring remains extremely high. The extent to which things are likely to change is difficult to assess, but it would seem probable that the carers of the future will have considerably greater expectations of individual rights and gender equalities of opportunity than do today's carers.

How Far Will They Go?: The Limits to Caring

Family commitment to care of elderly people is high today and, given the strength of traditions of family care, appears unlikely to change dramatically over the next few years. A key issue, Doty suggests, is "not only whether family members are available and willing to provide home care, but how much care and for how long?" (Doty, 1986: 47). While some carers "establish definite limits beyond which they will not go" at the onset of the care situation, many of them in all the European Union countries go beyond that limit, whatever the cost to themselves (Jani-Le Bris, 1993a: 73). Spouses, in particular, "show a strong tendency to maintain care giving whatever the social/emotional costs and stop only when deterioration in their own health physically prevents them from providing the services." (Doty, 1986: 51). American studies have suggested that it is deterioration in the health of the elderly dependent which is most likely to cause a breakdown in the caring relationship (Arling and McAuley, 1983; Smallegan, 1983, 1985), and acute situations involving sudden deterioration in functional ability have been found to be especially likely to precipitate an application for institutional admission (Harkins, 1985). Behavioural problems have been found especially difficult for carers to manage; Jani-Le Bris observes that "limits to caring are often conceived in terms of senile dementia or incontinence" (Jani-Le Bris, 1993a: 73).

Bearing in mind the high level of assistance already being provided and the fact that, in the absence of medical advance, the incidence of dementia is likely to increase significantly, it cannot be taken for granted that carers in the future will be either willing or able to care for their elderly relatives "until the bitter end." Without support, there is a high chance that tolerance levels for carers faced with the prospect of providing long-term care for very dependent elderly relatives will be stretched to the limit and service provision (either institutional placements or high-input domiciliary services) sought for increasing numbers of elderly people.

Support Needs

Assistance focused specifically on carers is rare in the European Union. The eleven national reports made clear that one of the most desired types of support among informal carers was respite care - the opportunity to take a break from caring while someone else looks after an elderly dependent. The Netherlands report observes that "one of the wishes most often expressed by carers is to have somebody take over the task of caring temporarily. This may mean that the person cared for is accommodated elsewhere for part of the week, but also that someone comes in to keep an eye on the person cared for at home, for example over the weekend." (Steenvoorden, 1993: 29).

Other expressed needs were for information and advice, the opportunity to talk to other people in similar situations to themselves, practical and financial assistance. If we are to ensure that carers do not 'reach the limits of caring' in the future, it is imperative that meeting these very specific and clearly articulated needs be incorporated into public policies.

Employment and Caring: Choice or Balance?

The increasing involvement of women in the European Labour Market has already been discussed, and (since quality of life of carers is as important an issue as availability) we now turn to the question of what women in the future are likely to *want* in terms of employment in the future; moving from a practical perspective to a normative and attitudinal one.

Leaving aside for a moment the much debated question of whether or not there is a conflict between employment and caring duties, it is important to emphasise the fact that a high proportion of people who give care to elderly people in Europe *do* combine their caring duties with work outside the home. It has been estimated that one in nine full-time workers and one in five part-time workers have caring responsibilities (for a sick, handicapped or elderly person) (Eurolink Age, 1993b: 17).

Evidence from the eleven national reports makes it clear that, for carers, paid employment serves two very important functions. Firstly, it has a "restorative" function to the extent that it allows the carer a respite from caring. The French report refers to "the general sense of balance conferred by work activity, the counterweight which work provided against the functions of being a carer, and having relationships outside the family." (Jani-Le Bris, 1993b: 65). One of the carers in the German study commented "My only hobby is my work. I only get out then." (Döhner *et al.*, 1993: 79). In the sense of acting in a "restorative" way work outside the home can allow individuals to maintain an identity other than that of 'carer' (Triantafillou and Mestheneos, 1993); allow personal enhancement (Jani-Le Bris, 1993a), provide social support (Naegele and Reichert, 1993) and act as a lifeline to counteract isolation (Rimmer and Popay, 1992).

Apart from affording carers the opportunity to balance their lives, work outside the home obviously fulfils a financial function; in many cases not only for the benefit of the carer. Askham *et al.* observed that "earnings from employment may enable some of the financial costs of caring to be met . . ." (Askham *et al.*, 1992: 79). The author of the Spanish national report observed that, while carers with a higher social status sought employment for a variety of non-financial reasons, for less well-off carers "it was their work that provided them with the means to support themselves and their parents" (Rodriguez, 1993: 41).

Employment or Caring: Is There a Conflict?

One question which has been much debated in recent years is that of whether or not women's increasing involvement in the labour market represents a 'threat' to informal care of elderly people.

In Britain, the majority of women of working age who provide care for elderly people do participate - at least to some extent - in the labour market. In the British General Household Survey of 1985, three-quarters of all carers aged 16 to 64 defined themselves as "economically active" and two-thirds said that they had paid jobs (Green, 1988). There is other (British) evidence to suggest that women who work are no less likely to provide care for an elderly relative than women who do not (Martin and Roberts, 1984) and that co-residence with an elderly relative is more common among women who work than among those who do not (Grundy and Harrop, 1992b).

On the other hand, data from Britain also shows that carers are less likely to be in paid employment than non-carers, with carers being more likely to work part time (Green, 1988). Numerous studies have found that significant proportions of informal carers state that they have found it necessary to give up their paid employment in order to be able to provide care (Martin and Roberts, 1984; Askham *et al.*, 1992: 39; Carers National Association, 1993; Glendinning and McLaughlin, 1993; Naegele and Reichert, 1993). Other studies have demonstrated the way in which caring responsibilities can affect work opportunities both at the time of caring (e.g. lost pay from unpaid time-off, work interruptions, having to change to less well paid but more convenient jobs, reduced hours of work, foregoing shift work and overtime opportunities) and later in life (e.g. loss of pension rights) (Nissel and Bonnerjea, 1982; Martin and Roberts, 1984; Brody *et al.*, 1987; Glendinning, 1992a & b; Eurolink Age, 1993a).

It appears that, while many carers do manage to continue working, the impact of caring on employment depends to a large extent on the intensity of assistance which is required and also varies according to gender, marital status and other demographic characteristics (Baldwin, 1985; Baldwin and Parker, 1991). The broad picture presented by these various studies would appear to be that, while there is no clear-cut conflict between working and care giving (and as noted above, employment outside the home can have positive benefits for carers), carers who do attempt to combine work and caregiving responsibilities are likely to suffer restrictions in their opportunities and may, especially where their caring duties are particularly heavy, have to give up work altogether.

As yet, only a few companies in a few Member States have had the foresight to instigate flexible working arrangements for people who provide care for elderly relatives. Job sharing, paid care leave, flexible hours, the opportunity to make private telephone calls; these and many other arrangements could all help working carers to combine their two very important roles (Askham *et al.*, 1992).

Carers and Employment: Looking to the Future

Bearing in mind that there can be conflicts between caregiving and working and the tendency for women to enter (or re-enter) the labour market after childbearing, what are the prospects for the future? Will an increasing number of women be entering the work force who might otherwise be available to provide care for elderly relatives?

With continuing changes in gender-role behaviour - including involvement in the labour force of women whose partners are unemployed and increasing awareness of the need for equality of opportunity in all dimensions of life - there seems little doubt that women will continue to *wish* to work. In terms of likely *actual* levels of labour force participation, however, this is much more difficult to estimate. Long term forecasts can be very unreliable - activity rates have changed greatly in the past and are likely to change further in the future, in response to a variety of factors which are not easy to predict accurately for long periods ahead. Activity rates in 20 years time will depend not only on the economic situation in individual states, but also on changing attitudes, facilities for flexible working arrangements and other factors.

Despite Europe's efforts over the last decade, full employment can no longer be taken for granted as the automatic outcome of growth-creating economic policies (Commission of the European Communities, 1993a). A recent European Social Policy document argues that "All the evidence points to deep underlying structural problems in Europe which makes a return to full employment unlikely for the foreseeable future unless significant changes in policy are introduced." (Commission of the European Communities, 1993a: 18). Already we are seeing changes to the "traditional" pattern of a forty-year working life, so that whatever women's participation rates in the future, paid work is likely to occupy less of their lives than was the case in the past.

Recent work suggests that women will continue to represent an increasing proportion of the European workforce. Using a 'high activity' scenario, it has been estimated that the proportion of women in the labour force will rise to around 45% in 2010; of the total increase in the numbers coming onto the market over this period, some 73% would be women. On a 'low activity/low population' projection, the importance of women would still increase over the next twenty years, but the rise would be much less. "Over the Community as a whole, the share of women would increase from 40% to around 42% in twenty years time, with little or no rise in a number of countries, such as Belgium, Luxembourg and France, and with Italy even showing a fall." (Commission of the European Communities, 1992b: 71). If the tendency for women to take part-time rather than full-time employment (which is particularly evident in the United Kingdom) turns out to be a cohort effect, and women in the future are attracted more to full time work, this could, indeed, have implications for the care of elderly relatives.

One of the crucial contradictions facing the welfare state in relation to care for elderly people is the dual role played by women within society and the economy (Bennington and Taylor, 1993). A recent OECD report recognised that one important means of seeking to increase the capacity of an economy to meet the demands of an ageing population is to increase labour force participation rates - and that one of the most important groups among whom such an increase is possible is women (OECD, 1988). However, as Bennington and Taylor (1993) point out, any increases in tax revenue resulting from women giving up unpaid caring roles and entering the labour force will have to be offset against the additional costs to the state of providing substitute care for the increased numbers of unsupported dependants.

Available Options: Alternative Sources of Care

The availability of alternative sources of care (e.g. public, private or voluntary services) in the future will undoubtedly have an effect not only on the family's *need* to provide care but also on its *willingness* to assist elderly relatives. Rather than replacing family care, services have been found rather to complement it, and British work has demonstrated the way in which service provision can enhance carers' willingness to continue caring, even in extremely difficult circumstances (Levin *et al.*, 1989).

Jani-Le Bris observes that community care services in all Member States are "either underdeveloped or overstretched, and never manage to meet the needs" (Jani-Le Bris, 1993a: 124). In Greece, Ireland, Italy, Portugal and Spain, community care services are relatively underdeveloped (Jani-Le Bris, 1993a; Walker *et al.*, 1993), while Belgium, Denmark, France, Germany, Luxembourg, the Netherlands and the United Kingdom have a number of home-based services but in insufficient supply (Jani-Le Bris, 1993a; Walker *et al.*, 1993). Only in Denmark is there a widespread 24-hour service. Walker observes that ". . . there is a continuing care gap and many home care services (in the European Union) are still stuck in a traditional mould . . . the signs of overburdening can be seen in the incidence of physical and mental ill-health among informal carers (and in sickness rates among paid home carers)" (Walker, 1992: 20).

In the face of financial restrictions and attempts to contain public spending, we cannot rely on substantial increases in service provision. The potential for changes of priority in resource allocation (e.g. from the acute sector to the long-term care sector) should not, however, be dismissed. It would seem that there is considerable scope for redistribution of resources.

The Balance of Service Provision: Public, Private and Voluntary

Apart from variations in the overall level of service provision, the balance of provision varies considerably between Member States. The future balance of care could have important implications for the provision of family support in the future; reductions in public provision for instance, would mean a likely increase for the roles of private and voluntary organisations and/or family carers.

In recent years, the role of the public sector as the main provider of social and health services has receded somewhat; but the state remains the dominant actor in Europe, especially in the medical and paramedical areas. In other aspects of community care - non-medical domiciliary services and day centres for example - the state may act as regulator, financier or initiator of services which may be delivered by other actors (Work Research Centre/EKOS, 1991).

In the sector of long-term care and home help services, provision of public services is generally strongly complemented by private or voluntary providers; Denmark being the only country with a marked predominance of public provision in counties or municipalities (Walker *et al.*, 1993). Voluntary associations are especially strong in Germany, Belgium and the Netherlands and church-based voluntary associations play important roles as providers of services in Greece, Ireland, Italy, Portugal and Spain (op cit).

Home care provision is predominantly state provided in Denmark (Schou *et al.*, 1993), dominated by charitable organisations in Germany (Jamieson, 1991), and in the UK provided mainly by the local authorities complemented by a small amount of private provision. In Greece, many middle class families make their own arrangements for the care of elderly relatives, in the absence of state provision, by employing immigrant labour.

In terms of institutional care, Denmark, France and Luxembourg report a predominantly public supply of facilities, while in Germany, Greece, the Netherlands and Portugal the bulk of residential care for the elderly is supplied by non-profit associations in the voluntary sector (Walker *et al.*, 1993). Belgium has a "fairly balanced structure of supply", with public, non-profit and private providers commanding almost equal shares of the residential industry. Italy and UK are the only countries with a predominance of private (including non-profit) supply (Walker *et al.*, 1993). Thus, across Europe there is considerable diversity of "welfare mix".

A recent report suggests that the increasing tendency towards market-orientation evident in many of the countries of the European Union is likely to continue. "The emergence of the so-called contract culture, whereby the state contracts the delivery of welfare provision to non-state organisations, is likely to increase the role of the private sector in the future" (Work Research Centre/EKOS, 1991: 52). This would certainly be in accordance with a recent tendency in many countries to place restrictions on state funding of services, and suggests that unless alternative arrangements are made to cover the cost of care provision (e.g. private long-term care insurance) informal carers are likely to be in a position of having to provide as much - if not more care than is currently the case unless they have the financial means necessary to buy alternative care.

Policy and Ideology

One clear policy emphasis in all Member States is on enabling people to remain at home for as long as possible (Jamieson, 1991; Jani-Le Bris, 1993a). This emphasis developed partly in response to the increasing numbers of elderly people in the populations of the European Union countries and partly as an attempt to control the growth in health and social expenditure, but the priority given to living at home coincides with the preferences of the majority of both elderly people and of their families (Jamieson, 1991; Jani-Le Bris, 1993a).

The extent to which families are expected to care for their elderly relatives, however, varies from state to state. Jamieson observes that ". . . in countries with a strong family ideology and where the state has historically played a residual role in social welfare, one can expect policies and service provision to be very different from that in countries with a more universalist welfare state" (Jamieson 1991: 248).

Informal carers (in particular families) are mentioned in policy statements of many of the European Union countries, "but in different ways that express some very important differences regarding the expected role of the family in providing care" (Jamieson, 1991: 241). Jamieson distinguishes three different 'ideal types' of state/ family responsibility balance. In the first, the state takes on responsibility for replacing the family, which is no longer expected to provide care for older relatives. In the second, the state fulfils a residual function, providing care only where there are no families available to do so. Finally, there is the situation in which the role of the state is seen as that of encouraging and supporting families by providing services which complement and support them so that their burden does not become so enormous that they totally relinquish their role (Jamieson, 1991). Utilising these different conceptions of the role of the state, it is possible to construct a broad "continuum of aims":

Replace informal care (e.g. Denmark) (Jamieson, 1991: 246)	- Support/Encourage informal care (e.g. UK, Netherlands)	- Provide a safety net for those with no informal networks (e.g. Germany, Italy)

At one end of the continuum we have Denmark, where there are laws specifically removing the responsibility for older relatives from the younger generation (Jani-Le Bris, 1993a: 11). Official Danish policy towards elderly people "does not consider the family's care of the elderly as a potential factor in the care of the elderly." (Schou *et al.*, 1993: 16) and largely because of this fact, the role of the family is hardly debated (Jamieson, 1991). The authors of the Danish report to the European Foundation observed that "neither the public sector nor society in general has given much attention to the role of relatives as carers" (Schou *et al.*, 1993: 23). Here, then, is an example of a country in which carers are not supported - or even really recognised - because their role in caring for elderly people is not officially acknowledged.

At the other end of the spectrum, there are several European countries in which families are made legally responsible for the care of older relatives. In Belgium, parents have a "maintenance obligation" for their children, spouses for one another and children to their parents (Hedebouw, 1993: 20). In France, the maintenance obligation constitutes the legal basis of the family's *de jure* liability to provide for the vital needs of its older members (Jani-Le Bris, 1993b: 18). In Germany, the responsibility of the family "is stated very explicitly in the principle of subsidiarity guiding social welfare." (Jamieson, 1991: 245). Here, families are obliged to provide either care or financial assistance towards care for frail relatives. Whereas in Denmark carers are absent from the policy agenda because they are not expected to play an important role, in Germany they are low on the political agenda because they are simply expected to fulfil their obligations to care (Jamieson, 1991: 289).

Jamieson suggests that the fact that informal carers are recognised in Britain, and are central to the policy agenda relates to some extent to the lack of consensus about their role (Jamieson, 1991). The authors of the UK Report to the European Foundation observe that "in the UK, the role of family carers has been given increasing prominence in the policy agenda over the past ten years" (Finch *et al.*, 1993: 34). Numerous policy documents have emphasised the central role of families in the care of older people, with public services acting to enable them to continue in this role (Finch *et al.*, 1993).

Policies for the Future?

In terms of the recognition of the role of - and policy to support - family carers, all Member States of the European Union have a very long way to go. So far only the UK, whose policy clearly envisages that family care will continue as a key component of provision for elderly people in the foreseeable future (Finch *et al.*, 1993), has come anywhere near to the formulation of a policy to support family carers (Jani-Le Bris, 1993a: 126), although other countries do provide financial support for family care. In the Netherlands, "there is no effective policy on the part of the government for the improvement of the conditions for providing family care" (Steenvoorden, 1993: 127), while the authors of the Greek report suggest that "given the current economic situation and the public sector deficit, it is unlikely that government policies will be directed towards new and specific services for the carers of the dependent elderly" (Triantafillou and Mestheneos, 1993: 80).

In Spain, while various policy documents may make it easier for families to care for their elderly relatives, there is no single policy whose direct aim is to help families with the needs and problems associated with caring for elderly people (Rodriguez, 1993). In Italy the economic advantages of family care for elderly people are recognised by the government (Mengani and Gagliardi, 1993), but there is no overall policy for supporting them in their task (Rodriguez, 1993).

The role of carers, then, is recognised to varying degrees in the different Member States of the European Union. Clearly, what is expected of families in the future will depend to a large extent on existing ideology. One would not, for example, expect that in Denmark, where there has been an explicit assumption that families will not care for their elderly relatives, there would be a sudden change of policy *towards* family responsibility (although it is assumed that spouses will provide care, and support is being developed for carers to some extent). In the same way, one would least expect a dramatic withdrawal of family care in countries such as Greece, where such care has traditionally been taken for granted and in those countries where there is a legal obligation to care for elderly relatives. The risk, however, is that existing traditions will serve as convenient carriers of the *status quo*. On the one hand, the needs of carers will continue to be unrecognised because they do not - officially - exist, while on the other, their needs will be ignored because they are, after all only "doing their duty". Unless the governments of Member States fully recognise the value of the contribution made by families, acknowledge the implications of the demographic and social changes which will take place over the next 20 years, and develop policies built upon them, there can be no guarantee that, in 20 years time, families will still be able - or willing - to care for their elderly relatives. In this case, individual states would be left to 'carry the can' and the quality of life of elderly people would probably deteriorate.

Economic Factors

Recession and the search for cheaper care

In all European Union Member States, economic concern about the cost implications of population ageing (in terms of pensions, health and social services) is coupled with political worries about the fiscal implications of increased welfare spending (Bak, 1989; Walker, 1992; Ferrera, 1993). As a result of economic pressures, attempts have been made to find cheaper forms of care. The UK, Germany and Denmark "all have in common the realisation by policy makers that health service expenditure cannot keep growing in an uncontrolled manner" (Jamieson, 1990: 17), so that even in Denmark (where the state takes full responsibility for caring for elderly people), financial pressures have led to restrictions in the provision of services. Here, the question has been "how can the municipalities care for an increasing number of the elderly in a period of declining resources (and at the same time maintain quality)" (Schou *et al.*, 1993: 68).

In the UK, a government document on services for elderly people stated categorically in 1981 that public authorities would not have sufficient resources to provide adequate support for elderly people without other input (cited in Parker, 1993: 6). Walker notes that, in general, economic concerns about the cost implications are universal in the European Union, but observes that "the most extreme forms of pessimism are associated primarily with those governments that, for ideological reasons, have adopted an anti-welfare state posture" (Walker, 1992: 15). While in most European Union countries, economic pressures give an impetus toward cost-effectiveness, in the extreme pessimistic form of these pressures "there is a desire to place even greater burdens on family members and to encourage the growth of the private and voluntary sectors in substitution for the public sector" (ibid).

In less pessimistic vein Hills (1993) has suggested that, at least in Britain, the 'demographic time bomb' has been exaggerated. He argues that the total net effects of the ageing population and higher basic pension entitlements on Britain's public finances over the next fifty years would add up to about 5% of Gross Domestic Product - no more than the increase mainly due to the recession over the past three years.

In the search for cost-effectiveness, which will undoubtedly continue, "community care" is likely to constitute a central policy aim, on the now well established assumption that keeping elderly people at home is cheaper than institutional care. The danger is that, in this search, families are likely to be "taken for granted", as they have been traditionally in the vast majority of the European Union states, and that governments will fail to recognise the full implications of the dramatic social and demographic changes which are taking place. Governments have never been good at 'spending now to save in the future' but that is precisely what is required. If money is not spent now on supporting family carers, the cost implications for the governments of the future - to say nothing of the cost to families' and elderly people's quality of life - could be enormous.

Competing Demands for Resources

Especially in times of economic strictures, competing demands on public resources may force down the public expenditure allocation to elderly people and their families. A recent OECD report suggests that "the ageing of populations is likely to increase the demand for pensions, for health care and for other social services catering to the needs of the elderly, while demographic pressures on education systems and other services utilised mainly by the young may decrease." (OECD 1988: 27). The cost of education, however, may not fall significantly if an increasing proportion of teenagers stay on at school or go on to further or higher education or training.

A more likely - and substantial - drain on Member States' economies will be unemployment. Since the beginning of the 1970s unemployment in the European Union has risen steadily, except during the second half of the 1980s (Commission of the European Communities, 1993c). Unemployment doubled from 8 million in 1980 to 16 million in 1987, and since then the aggregate is downwards (Work Research Centre/EKOS, 1991). Only in four countries, however, (Belgium, Spain, the Netherlands and the UK) is there a clear trend towards lower rates of unemployment - in other Member States there is either a continued increase or only very recent indications of a downturn. Even more significant in regard to public expenditure is the proportion of long term unemployed among the unemployed generally; in the European Union as a whole there has been an increase in long-term unemployment and in 1989 over half the unemployed had been out of work for one year or more (op cit). High rates of unemployment and long-term unemployment "require substantial state spending on training, counselling and welfare provision" (Work Research Centre/EKOS, 1991: 56).

Demands for resources arising from developments in medical science and technology are infinite and Jamieson observes that the increase in spending on health in advanced industrial societies is "very much a consequence of this rather than of any planned and carefully worked out priorities" (Jamieson, 1990: 17). Jamieson goes on to suggest that, "if more involvement of the family in caring for the elderly is seen as necessary, *it is mainly due to lack of will or inability to shift priorities in the direction of primary health care and social care.*" (ibid) (emphasis added).

There are radical questions to be answered here. Are our expenditure priorities appropriate for current society's needs? How will they need to be changed if we are to meet the social needs of the future?

The Effect of the "Unpredictable"

Apart from the demographic projections of the likely numbers of people in different age groups in the future, all of the factors which have been discussed in relation to the potential future supply of family care for elderly people are, to varying degrees, impossible to project with any level of accuracy. One can only guess, for example, how attitudes towards caring for elderly relatives are likely to change in the next 20 years. There are however some events which, while impossible to predict, have considerable potential for affecting the future of family care for elderly people. The onset of large-scale warfare could make heavy demands on the economies of Member States, as could environmental disasters. Either of these occurrences would almost certainly increase the demands made upon families to provide care for their elderly relatives.

Summary: The Potential Supply of Family Care for Elderly People

1. Despite occasional suggestions to the contrary, families in the European Union provide the majority of care for elderly people, often at considerable cost to themselves.

2. The continuing decline in fertility rates throughout the European Union will have the consequence, from the second decade of the next century, of reducing the number of "next generation" women (who represent a high proportion of carers) in relation to the numbers of elderly people likely to require care.

3. The increasing tendency for couples to live together, rather than marrying, and increasing divorce rates are likely to blur the lines of responsibility for the care of elderly relatives.

4. Many carers in the future (as at present) will themselves be elderly and will be likely to suffer from similar health problems to those of the elderly population as a whole.

5. While there would not appear to be a clear cut conflict between care giving and paid employment, attempting to combine these two roles can be problematic. The chances are high that women in the European Union will continue to wish to enter (or re-enter) the labour force after childbearing and if there is a high demand for full-time employment without the provision of flexible working arrangements, this could have the effect of reducing the availability of family care.

6. In general, families have high levels of commitment to caring for elderly relatives, even in countries where family care is not a legal requirement. However, caring can have severe physical, psychological, emotional and financial costs, and the likely increase in dementia among the elderly population is likely to increase significantly the demands made upon a diminishing number of carers.

7. Among carers' reported support needs in the European Union, the need for respite care, information and advice and the opportunity to share experiences with others in the same situation figure prominently. As yet, these needs are met only to a very limited extent in Europe.

8. All Member States of the European Union espouse policies of 'community care'. As yet, however, support for family carers (on whom such policies depend) fails to figure prominently on policy agendas, suggesting that very few - if any - Member States have yet acknowledged the

implications of social and demographic changes for the future care of elderly people.

9. With increasing pressure on budgets, the search is on for cheaper forms of care for elderly people. There is a danger that families will continue to be "taken for granted" in the attempt to keep costs down.

CHAPTER 4 CONCLUSIONS AND OPTIONS FOR THE FUTURE

Conclusions

Throughout the European Union there is wide diversity, not only in the level of service provision for elderly people, but also in the expectations of family care, the degree of recognition of the role of family carers, and the extent to which the needs of these individuals are recognised and met. This diversity is likely to be increased with the entry into the EU of Finland, Austria, Norway and Sweden. Setting aside these differences between Member States, however, all face similar demographic changes over the next twenty years and similar challenges to action.

The future potential for family care of older people in the European Union depends on a host of factors, many of them interacting and most of them likely to be subject to considerable variability in the future. It is not possible, as a result of these analyses, to present a precise picture of the future, but it is clear that well-grounded discussion at European and State level concerning policies for the future care of elderly people are urgently needed.

Figure 2 summarises the main factors which have emerged from the analysis as likely to affect future demands for and future supply of family care for older people in Europe.

Of greatest concern is the fact that although the numbers of potential carers will increase relative to the number of elderly people over the next few years (due to the ageing of those who gave birth during the baby boom years), during the second decade of the next century we will really begin to see the effect of falling fertility rates in Europe. There will be many more elderly people in twenty years' time than there are now and, in particular, more very elderly people who have the highest care needs. Many are likely to require care over long time periods and the incidence of dementia is likely to increase. Rising divorce rates have the potential to blur the lines of family responsibility, while increases in the rate of employment of women - in the absence of flexible working arrangements - would reduce the number of available carers.

Figure 2:
Care in the balance: main factors likely to affect future demand for and supply of family care to older people in Europe

	DEMAND FOR FAMILY CARE	**SUPPLY OF FAMILY CARE-GIVERS**
Factors with potential to increase demand/ reduce supply	• Increase in numbers of elderly people relative to carers • Increase in chronic illness • Increase in dementia • More very elderly people	• Higher female employment rates • Higher rates of divorce and remarriage • Increased internal and external migration
Factors with potential to decrease demand/ increase supply	• Improved health due to preventive health care/changes in health behaviour/ developments in technology • Increasing preference for state, rather than family, care • Political pressure for higher levels of service provision • Long-term care insurance	• Policies to support carers
Factors with potential to increase or decrease	• Level of service provision and financial support	• Level of service provision and financial support • Health status of carers

Among the elderly populations of the future, elderly women will be especially at risk of neglect, for many of them are likely to be widowed, to have high dependency needs, and to be living alone on low incomes. Also at risk will be those who, without occupational or private pensions, are not able to purchase the care they need and must rely on an overburdened welfare state or on their families for care. Less dependent elderly people who rely on a number of different family members to help them may be at special risk of loss of assistance. Whereas younger relatives caring for very family dependent elderly people may be less likely to abandon their task, those providing just a few hours' help a week may be the ones most likely to withdraw their support.

However, the chances of huge increases in formal service provision are extremely low. In some of the European Union countries, provision is still at a very low level, and even in those states considered comparatively well provided, service provision is often patchy, inflexible and poorly co-ordinated, with informal carers constituting a huge, still largely unacknowledged army of support. Despite suggestions to the contrary, families still give a very great deal of assistance to elderly people in the European Union; providing by far the majority of support. Policies of community care, espoused by the governments of all Member States, assume the continuation of this support, yet nowhere have the full implications of social and demographic changes for families providing care been recognised.

If factors with the potential to increase demand for care (increasing numbers of elderly people, increases in chronic illness and an increasing proportion of very elderly people) exert their maximum effects in combination with factors having the potential to reduce the supply of care (higher female employment, higher rates of divorce and remarriage and increased migration), we will be faced, in twenty years' time, with a 'crisis of care' unlike anything Europe has experienced in the past.

If we are to ensure the quality of life of tomorrow's elderly people, it cannot - and must not - be assumed that families will continue to be willing and able to provide current levels of support to elderly relatives in the future. At the same time, it would be foolhardy to assume that, 20 years from now, individual states will somehow "find a way" to support their elderly populations. What is required, it seems, is a way of thinking towards policy which does not conceptualise the solution to the question in terms of "either"/"or" - *either* services *or* families. There is a need for a much higher level of partnership than currently exists; a realisation that, if community care policies are to be anything other than a cheaper alternative to institutional care, the irreplaceable role of families must be acknowledged and their contributions fostered.

At present neither elderly people nor their carers have any real degree of choice in terms of what is provided or by whom. This is the situation from which we should be aiming to break away. If choice be accepted as a basic principle of citizenship, then it is essential that we seek to move towards the situation in which family care for elderly people is provided by people who have the freedom to decide for themselves what their contribution will be. In looking ahead over the next twenty years, our concern must be not simply with the costs of caring for an increasing European population of elderly people and with the sustainability of family care, but also with the preservation of quality of life, both for elderly people and for their family carers.

Options for the Future

With projections of many more elderly people in the Europe of the future and the probable constraints on the provision of family care, there is an urgent need for the governments of the Member States to recognise just how much they currently depend on informal carers - many of whom are themselves elderly - and to consider all possible options in making solid plans for the future. There is an urgent need for better information to allow planning for the future and in particular in order to be able to prepare for the large increase associated with the coming of the 'baby boom' cohorts into old age.

Further research is required in three specific areas:

Provision of Basic Information on the Situation of Family Carers in the European Union

In most of the Member States, there is a pressing need for nationally representative research on the socio/ demographic and socio/cultural characteristics of carers, their needs and the assistance they provide to elderly people (Jani-Le Bris, 1993a).

Evaluation of the Effects of Policies and Initiatives to Support Family Carers

Once base level information has been obtained, it will then be possible to undertake research to ascertain the effect of initiatives and policies on the quality of life of elderly people and their carers. Specific information is requested on:

- the costs and effectiveness of public policies for the care o& elderly people
- the economic value of care provided by families and the economic costs incurred
- the costs and effectiveness of specific service interventions including detailed analysis of the benefits/ costs to carers
- the acceptability and likely effects of financial incentives versus service provision for family carers (including the effects of such incentives on the quality of family relationships).

Research on Attitudes to Receipt of - and Provision of - Family Care

In many Member States there is a shortage of research on preferences for care among people of all ages. It is important that such research be promoted, and that the results of such research be interpreted within the existing sociocultural context. Comparative international research - particularly of a longitudinal nature - would be particularly fruitful.

Presented below are four 'options' which may be considered in approaching the issue of future care for elderly people. Family care is not, and should not be, the only option considered.

1. Reducing Demand for Care: A Preventive Approach

One strategy for the future could be an attempt to reduce the demand for care by focusing on improving elderly people's health and independence.

Development of Preventive Health Care and Information Programmes

Early detection of eyesight, hearing and foot problems, and encouraging people to adopt healthier lifestyles could have considerable potential for reducing morbidity and increasing mobility and independence in old age. Consideration would have to be given to inequalities among the elderly population in terms of access to services and information.

Housing Strategies

Housing policy can have very significant implications for elderly people's ability to live independently; an OECD report published in 1990 notes that "housing policies are seen as critical links in formulating integrated responses to the problems of long-term care" (OECD, 1990b: 5). Elderly people's housing is often inappropriate in terms of design and operating costs and in many countries there is a shortage of suitable housing - in particular, of small units of accommodation (OED, 1990a, 1990b). Granny flats, where an elderly person and a family can live side-by-side, can enable elderly people to maintain their independence yet have help at hand (Tinker, 1991), while for elderly people with disabilities who need more support than can be provided in non-specialised housing, congregate or sheltered housing with extra care can provide a satisfactory solution (Tinker, 1989).

Bearing in mind the potential specialised housing can have for elderly peoples' independence, attempts should be made to develop social and housing policy for elderly people in an integrated manner, with special attention being given to the development of small, purpose-built or specially-adapted living units.

Development of "Assistive Technology"

There are many technological devices - many of them comparatively simple and inexpensive - which have high potential for enabling elderly people to live independently in their own homes. Mobility aids, alarms, telephone links, etc., could all enhance disabled people's ability to care for themselves. Bearing in mind that there will be more very elderly people in the future, and that willingness to use this technology is likely to increase, serious consideration should be given to research and development in this area.

Creating, Extending and/or Restructuring Home Care Services

At present, most home care services (even where they are available) tend to be inflexible, and to provide standardised - rather than tailor-made - care. Attempts should be made to ensure that home care services reach those most in need of them, and that they are able to respond in a flexible way to individual need.

Services for Independence

Some heath and social services which are aimed at maintaining or restoring independence in old age can enhance elderly people's ability to continue living in their own home. Health expenditure priorities for services such as physiotherapy, speech and occupational therapy should be reviewed.

Encouraging self-sufficiency

Encouraging elderly people's self-help skills (e.g. teaching widowed people, who have always relied on their partner to perform what they saw as gender-appropriate roles, how to do those things for themselves) and encouraging elderly people to form groups to help one another - e.g. to run telephone advice lines or provide assistance - would not only make people more independent but would capitalise on their skills and knowledge. Consideration should be given to the development of self-sufficiency training programmes for elderly people living alone or with a disabled elderly partner.

Reallocation of Resources

There would appear to be considerable scope, in many countries, for moving resources from acute care towards primary and long term care. Bearing in mind the increasing size of the elderly population in the European Union, consideration should be given to the possibility of moving health and social care resources from "curing" to "caring".

Implications

What could be the implications of a focus upon the maintenance of physical fitness and independence in the elderly populations of the future? In the absence of significant developments in research on dementia, one outcome could be an increase in the number of elderly people who are physically fit but mentally frail. This could significantly change the nature of the caring task. Future developments in technology may ensure that elderly people's physical needs are more fully met, but could lead to an increasing need for emotional support.

With increasing reliance on technology, isolation and loneliness (already a problem for many elderly people) could increase and emergency cover in the event of technical breakdown would be essential. Access to home aids and technology would undoubtedly vary considerably according to income. Provision of such developments for elderly people in isolated rural areas could be especially helpful in ensuring their security and well-being, but the ethical implications of home monitoring systems would require serious consideration. Questions of 'acceptable risk' and discrepancies between what is acceptable to elderly people and to care professionals and families would require discussion.

With higher levels of mobility, more elderly people would be able to utilise services provided outside the home, and would increase wealth by their spending on goods and services. Greater independence and better health could also enhance family solidarity by enabling elderly people to care for grandchildren while their adult children go out to work.

2. Stimulating Supply: Supporting Carers

At present, support of any kind for carers is poorly developed in Europe. There are few services designed specifically to meet their needs, little formal financial support to compensate them for their input and few facilities to meet their emotional and training needs. Where community services are provided they are usually focused primarily on the needs of the elderly dependant, so that the abilities and needs of family members are considered of only secondary importance.

A complementary approach to meeting the care needs of elderly people in the future could focus on the development of flexible mixed welfare arrangements which would not only make it easier for families to provide care for elderly relatives but would consider their needs alongside those of their dependants.

Developing Family Based Policies for the Elderly

Assistance for family carers should form an integral part of the objectives and responsibilities of services and organisations looking after elderly people; Member States should be encouraged to develop health and social policies for elderly people which take into account the needs of family carers.

Family Centred Services

At present, most health and social services provided for elderly people focus specifically on the needs of the elderly person and providers frequently make assumptions concerning the availability of family care. Consideration needs to be given to making health and social services provision family-focused to the extent that need assessment is based on the needs of the family as a whole, building on its strengths and supporting its weaknesses.

Developing co-operation and co-ordination between different care providers (including principal carers)

There is a need to ensure the co-ordination of care for individual elderly people, ensuring complete care coverage, reducing overlaps and taking into account both the preferences of the dependent person and the abilities and preferences of the family carer/s. Where one family member is providing the majority of care, consideration should be given to encouraging input from other available family members. Consideration should be given to development of "key workers" for elderly dependants and their families, to co-ordinate care and ensure complete care coverage, taking carer needs very much into account.

Provision of Respite and Other Support Services

Families are better able to tolerate the long-term stress of caring for a disabled elderly person - especially one suffering some form of dementia or with heavy personal care assistance needs - if they are able to obtain periodic respite (Doty, 1986). The possibility of having a regular break from caring was one of the needs most frequently mentioned by carers in the eleven European Foundation reports.

Respite care can take many forms, including "granny sitting", day centres, temporary residential care, holiday stays for dependent people, temporary fostering (with another family member or someone unrelated to the elderly person).

It is important that such alternative care arrangements should be highly visible and accessible; carers need reassurance that, should there come a time when they are unable to continue caring, alternative care will be available at short notice.

There is a need to review respite care provisions and (where they exist) evaluate them in terms of costs and benefits to elderly people and carers; and for consideration to be given to the further development of such services - to be provided on a regular basis where required - to prevent the overburdening of carers. The provision of other services such as home nursing, home care, meal-provision and day-centres can be invaluable in supporting informal carers in their tasks.

Provision of Financial Support for Carers

Family carers are often financially disadvantaged in numerous ways, not only at the time of care giving but also, frequently, later in life. Consideration should be given to the possibility of providing financial assistance in respect of :
- recognition of the value of the work undertaken
- realistic compensation for forfeited employment opportunities (including pension entitlement cover for periods of care giving)
- expenses connected with the dependant (e.g. medical and paramedical costs, purchase/rental of minor equipment and technical resources - e.g. wheelchairs, walking frames)
- tax incentives for families taking elderly relatives into their home.

Introduction of Flexible Employment Arrangements

At present many women experience some degree of conflict between caring, care giving and paid employment. There is a need for the development of measures which would give them a real choice between various options. At one level, they need to be able to decide whether to remain in employment, reduce or stop work; at another level they need to be assured of a greater level of flexibility - where they choose to work - to combine their two roles. Consideration should be given to:
- the provision of alternative care arrangements for the dependent person to enable carers wishing to undertake paid employment to do so
- the establishment of flexible working hours/job sharing for carers

- the establishment of paid leave for carers, with coverage of rights to pension and sickness benefits
- guaranteed (or priority re-employment)
- assured social insurance rights (to cover illness and old age) where it is necessary to reduce hours or give up work due to carer responsibilities

Provision of Training and Information for Carers

Most carers take on the job of caring for elderly dependants with no specialist knowledge or training. They have to learn as they go, frequently at considerable cost to their physical and psychological health and at considerable economic expense. Special training in practical, psychological and emotional aspects of care can lead to improvements in their quality of life and greater satisfaction in the situation and relationship to care (Jani-Le Bris, 1993a: 136).

Apart from training programmes, information on the problems of old age needs to be provided in books, leaflets, television programmes, videos and local advice centres. Elderly people and their carers also need to be fully informed about the services and financial support available to them. For choice to exist, people have to know what is available to them. There is a need for consideration to be given to the review, evaluation and development of training programmes and information sources to family carers.

Encouraging and Supporting the Creation of Associations of Carers (National and Local) and Support Groups

Associations of carers (such as have been developed in recent years in Britain) can assist carers by allowing them to articulate their common needs and exert pressure on Governments to meet these needs. Carer groups have been found to provide valuable support to family carers, especially where psychological support and information is provided with some professional input. The development of carers associations (at national and local level) and carers support groups should therefore be encouraged.

Implications

While family carers in Europe have always provided the bulk of care for elderly people, their roles as 'carers' have not been fully or formally acknowledged. Taking their needs and abilities into account as part of a 'care package' would, to some extent at least, formalise their roles and have the potential to alter the relationship between them and their elderly dependants.

In a similar way, any form of financial support for informal carers could change the carer - dependant relationship.

The question of to whom such allowances should be paid (to carer or dependant) would clearly have to be addressed, taking into account the full implications of either option. If the dependants themselves were to be the recipients (as would be advocated by the disability lobby - see Morris, 1991), and their freedom of choice of care the primary concern, then real choices would have to exist for them. If the money were to be paid to the informal carer, consideration would have to be given to the possibility of exploitation and abuse.

As noted above, some elderly people and family carers will have considerably more scope for choice of care than others, due to better financial resources. It would therefore be essential that the question of how to ensure equality of access to services and of care options be fully considered.

Informal carers are not uniform in their needs for support. Spouse carers, many of whom will be elderly themselves, will require different forms of support than sons and daughters; male carers will require different types of help from female carers.

Acceptance of help from outside the family is likely to vary considerably between and within countries. Where there is a tradition of state welfare provision there may be little stigma attached to accepting service help; where there is no such tradition there may be a need for different support mechanisms.

If service provision is developed, the caring professions may become more vociferous in their demands for improved conditions, salaries and training. The EU countries, varying as they do in their experiences of care provision, have much to learn from one another in terms of the development of support mechanisms. There is a need to seek out and disseminate information on good practice.

3. Alternative Approaches to Care in the Community

The options so far discussed focus, firstly, upon reducing demand for care among future elderly populations by improving health and independence and, secondly, upon providing adequate support to enable and encourage families to provide care for elderly relatives. A third way of addressing the issue of future care for elderly people is to attempt to think beyond existing structures towards other ways in which care needs could be met.

Alternative ways of meeting elderly people's needs could include:

- intergenerational housing schemes (as has been developed in Spain: see Commission of the European Communities, 1993d)
- "service exchanges" at which elderly people can pay for the assistance they need with their own time and skills, rather than money.
- incentives for family members living apart to form family groups
- "surrogate" families in which elderly people without relatives can live with families in exchange for payment for rent and care provided.

Implications

Focusing upon what elderly people have to *give*, as well as on their support needs, will be vital in the future. Within that diverse and increasingly large group will be a wealth of knowledge, skills and experience.

With 'grey power' increasing in Europe and increasing expectations of quality of life, new forms of care and support will be required which capitalise on the valuable resources of the over-60s. Elderly people themselves can be instrumental in discussing and designing new ways of meeting their needs.

4. A New Face for Institutional Care?

It is important to recognise that the antipathy to institutional care which emerges so clearly from the literature on care preferences is based on individuals' perceptions and experiences of particular *forms* of institutional care. The development today of alternative forms of institutional care could alter the perceptions of tomorrow's elderly people to the extent that they enter individual consciousness as desirable and accessible options.

With greater awareness of individual rights, higher demands for a good quality of life and less willingness (or need) to accept what appears to be the 'only viable alternative', the face of residential care could change considerably. Many older people will continue to need (and some to prefer) residential care, even on today's design. Discussion of the ways in which it might develop in the future should accompany consideration of other options.

Inevitably, provision is all Member States is moving towards a 'welfare mix' of providers and options for care. There is a need to strengthen the debate by moving from an 'either/or' approach towards a concern with balance and a consideration of the quality of life for both older people and their carers.

REFERENCES

Arling G & McAuley W J (1983), The Feasibility of Public Payments for Family Caregiving, *Gerontologist*, **23**, pp 300-6.

Askham A, Grundy E & Tinker A (1992), Caring: *The Importance of Third Age Carers*, Research Paper No.6, Carnegie Inquiry into the Third Age, Carnegie United Kingdom Trust, Dunfermline, Scotland.

Askham J & Thompson C (1990), *Dementia and Home Care: A Research Report on a Home Support Scheme for Dementia Sufferers*, Research Paper No.4, Age Concern England/Age Concern Institute of Gerontology, King's College, London.

Bak M (1989), Introduction, in Boh K, Bak M Clason C et al, *Changing Patterns of European Family Life*, Routledge, London.

Bennington J & Taylor M (1993), Changes and challenges facing the UK Welfare State in the Europe of the 1990s. *Policy & Politics* 21(2), 121-134.

Boh K (1989), European Family Life Patterns - A Reappraisal, Chapter 13 in Boh K, Bak M, Clason C et al, *Changing Patterns of European Family Life*, Routledge, London.

Brody E M et al (1987), Work Status and Parent Care: A Comparison of Four Groups of Women, *The Gerontologist*, 27, 201-208

Bruder J, Klusmann D, Lauter H & Luders I (1981), *Relationships between Patients and their Family Carers in the Case of Chronic Illness at an Advanced Age*, Report for the German Research Association, Hamburg (cited in Dohner et al 1993).

Carers National Association (1993), *Counting the Costs of Caring*, Carers National Association, London.

CBGS (1975), *Survey of the Elderly*, (cited in Hedebouw, 1993, p.19).

CBGS (1985), *Survey of the Elderly*, (cited in Hedebouw, 1993, p.19).

Cicirelli V (1983), A Comparison of Helping Behaviour to Elderly Parents of Adult Children with Intact & Disrupted Marriages, *The Gerontologist*, 23, 619-625.

Coleman P & Bond J (1990), Ageing in the Twentieth Century, pp 11-16, in Bond J & Coleman P (eds), *Ageing in Society*, Sage Publications, London.

Commission of the European Communities (1992a), *Report from the Commission on the Application in the Member States of the Council Recommendation* 82/857/EEC of 10 December 1982 on the principles of a Community policy whith regard to retirement age, Brussels.

Commission of the European Communities (1992b), *Employment in Europe*, Office for Official Publications of the European Communities, Luxembourg.

Commission of the European Communities (1993a), *European Social Policy, Options for the Union*, Green Paper, Consultative Document, Commission of the European Communities, Luxembourg.

Commission of the European Communities (1993b), *Social Europe. 1993: European Year of Older People & Solidarity between Generations*, Office for Official Publications of the European Communities, Luxembourg.

Commission of the European Communities (1993c), *Growth, Competitiveness, Employment: The Challenges and Ways Forward into the 21st Century*, White Paper, Office for Official Publications of the European Communities, Luxembourg.

Commission of the Eurpean Communities (1993d), *European Networks of Innovative Projects Concerning Older People*, Working Document, Directorate-General V; Employment, Industrial Relations and Social Affairs.

Crimmins E M, Saito Y & Ingegneri D (1989), Changes in Life Expectancy & Disability-Free Life Expectancy in the United States, *Population & Development Review*, **15**, 2, 235-267.

Crosby G (ed.) (1993), *The European Directory of Older Age*, Centre for Policy on Ageing, London

Daatland S (1990), What are Families For? On Family Solidarity & Preference for Help, *Ageing & Society,* **10**, 1-15.

DaneAge Foundation (N/D), *New Horizons - New Elderly,* DaneAge Foundation's Study on the Future Elderly, Copenhagen, Denmark.

Döhner M, Rub H & Schick B (1993), *Family Care of the Older Elderly: Germany,* Working Paper No WP/93/18/EN, European Foundation for the Improvement of Living and Working Conditions, Dublin.

Dontas A S, Hollis-Triantifillou J & Mestheneos E (1990), *Policy & Services for the Elderly in Greece,* Center of Studies of Age-Related Change in Man, Athens.

Dooghe G (1992), *The Ageing of the Population in Europe: Socio - Economic Characteristics of the Elderly Population,* Garant Publishers, Leuven, Belgium.

Dooghe G (1993), *Demographic Aspects of Active Ageing in Europe,* Paper at Active Ageing in the 21st Century Conference, Valletta, Malta, 13-16 December.

Doty P (1986), *Family Care of the Elderly: The Role of Public Policy*, The Millbank Quarterly, **64**, 1, 34-75.

Eurolink Age (1993a), *A European Community Health Policy for Older People,* Eurolink Age, London.

Eurolink Age (1993b), *Caring: A European Issue?,* Eurolink Age Bulletin, July 1993.

European Foundation for the Improvement of Living & Working Conditions (1989), *Four Year Rolling Programme 1989-1992. 1992 & Beyond: New Opportunities for Action to Improve Living & Working Conditions in Europe,* Office for Official Publications of the European Communities, Luxembourg.

Eurostat (1990), *Inequality & Poverty in Europe,* Luxembourg.

Eurostat (1991), *Demographic Statistics 1991,* Statistical Office of the European Communities, Luxembourg.

Eurostat (1993a), *Demographic Statistics 1993,* Statistical Office of the European Communities, Luxembourg.

Eurostat (1993b), *Rapid Reports: Population & Social Conditions,* Luxembourg.

Evers A (1992), *Further Research in the Area of Collective Support Systems: Some Comments & Recommendations,* Paper at Conference on Past, Current & Future Initiatives on Ageing, Economic & Social Research Council, London, 20-21 May.

Ferrera M (1993), *EC Citizens & Social Protection: Main Results from a Eurobarometer Survey,* Commission of the European Communities, Div. V/E/2, Brussels.

Finch J (1984), *Community Care: Developing Non-Sexist Alternatives,* Critical Social Policy, 9 (cited in Morris 1991).

Finch J (1989), *Family Obligations & Social Change,* Polity Press, Cambridge.

Finch J & Mason J (1990a), Filial Obligations & Kin Support for Elderly People, *Ageing & Society,* 10, 151-175.

Finch J & Mason J (1990b), Gender, Employment & Responsibilities to Kin, *Work, Employment & Society,* 4, 3, 349-367.

Finch J & Mason J (1992), *Negotiating Family Responsibilities,* Tavistock/Routledge, London.

Finch J, Hugman R & Carter J (1993), *Family Care of the Older Elderly: United Kingdom,* Working Paper No WP/93/22/EN, European Foundation for the Improvement of Living & Working Conditions, Dublin.

Fries J F (1980), 'Ageing, Natural Death and the Compression of Morbidity', *New England Journal of Medicine,* 303 (3), 130-5.

Fries J F (1989), 'Reduction of the National Morbidity' in Lewis S (ed), *Ageing & Health,* Michigan, Lewis, pp 3-22.

Glendinning C (1992a), *The Costs of Informal Care: Looking Inside the Household,* HMSO, London.

Glendinning C (1992b), Employment & "Community Care": Policies for the 1990's, *Work, Employment & Society,* **6**, 1, 103-111.

Glendinning C & McLaughlin E (1993), *Paying for Care: Lessons from Europe,* Social Security Advisory Committee, Research Paper 5, London, HMSO.

Green H (1988), *General Household Survey 1985: Informal Carers,* HMSO, London.

Grimley Evans J, Goldacre M, Hodkinson M, Lamb S & Savory M (1992), *Health: Abilities and Wellbeing in the Third Age.* Research Paper No.9. The Carnegie Inquiry into the Third Age. Carnegie UK Trust.

Grundy E & Harrop A (1992a), Demographic Aspects of Ageing in Europe in Anderson R, Daunt P, Drury E et al, *The Coming of Age in Europe: Older People in the European Community,* Age Concern England, London.

Grundy E & Harrop A (1992b), Co-Residence Between Adult Children and their Elderly Parents in England & Wales, *Journal of Social Policy,* **21**, 3, 325-348.

Guardian, The (1994), 'Old Age Rebels with a Cause', *Guardian 'Society',* 18 May, p12.

Hafner H (1986), *Mental Health in Old Age,* Gustav Fischer, Stuttgart, New York, cited in Dohner et al 1993.

Harkins E (1988), *Family Support & Costs of Services for the Frail Elderly: Final Report,* HCFA Grant No 18-P-98080/3, Virginia Center on Aging, Virginia Commonwealth University, Richmond, Virginia (cited in Doty 1986).

Harris C (1983), *The Family & Industrial Society,* Allen & Unwin, London.

Healthy Ageing (1990), cited in Dooghe 1992.

Hedebouw G (1993), *Family Care of the Older Elderly: Belgiue,* Working Paper No WP/93/19/EN, European Foundation for the Improvement of Living & Working Conditions, Dublin.

Hills J (1993), The Future of Welfare: A Guide to the Debate, Joseph Rountree Foundation, York.

Hobman D (ed) (1993), Uniting Generations: Studies in Conflict and Co-operation, ASge Concern England, London.

Hoskins I (1993), Combining Work and Care for the Elderly: An Overview of the Issues, International Labout Review, 132, 3, 347-369.

Infratest Sozialforschung (1993), Hilfe-und Pflegebedürftige in privaten Haushalten, Endbericht zur Repräsentetiveheburg im Rahmen des Forschungsprojekts "Möglichkeiten und Grenzen der Selbständigen Lebensführung".

Institute for Bioethics/The Hasting Center (1993), What do we owe the Elderly?, Institute for Bioethics, Maastricht, The Netherlands & The Hastings Center, New York, USA.

Jamieson A (1990), Informal Care in Europe, Chapter One in Jamieson & Illsley R (eds) Contrasting European Policies for the Care of Older People. Avebury, Aldershot.

Jamieson A (ed.) (1991), Home Care for Older People in Europe: A Comparison of Policies & Practices, Oxford University Press, Oxford.

Jani-Le Bris H (1993a), Family Care of Dependent Older People in the European Community, European Foundation for the Improvement of Living and Working Conditions, Dublin.

Jani-Le Bris H (1993b), Family care of Older Elderly: France, Working Paper No. WP/93/17/EN, European Foundation for the Improvement of Living and Working Conditions, Dublin.

Johnson M L (1993), Generation Relations under Review, Chapter One in Hobman D (ed.).

Kelly R (1994), No easy answer to 21st-century pensions finding. The Guardian 14.3.94.

Kendig H (1986), Intergenerational Exchange in Kendig H (ed.) *Ageing & Families,* Allen & Unwin, Sydney, Australia (cited in Sundstrom [in press]).

Kraan R J, Baldock J, Davies B et al (1991), *Care for the Elderly: Significant Innovations in Three European Countries,* Campus Verlag, Frankfurt & Westview Press, Colorado.

Levin E, Sinclair I and Gorbach P (1989), *Families, Services & Confusion in Old Age,* Avebury, Aldershot.

Manton K G (1982), 'Changing Concepts of Morbidity and Mortality in the Elderly Population', Milbank Memorial Fund Quarterly, *Health & Society,* 60 (2) 183-244.

Martin J, Meltzer H & Elliot D (1988), *The Prevalence of Disability among Adults,* OPCS Surveys of Disability in Britain, Report 1, HMSO, London.

Martin J & Roberts C (1984), *Women & Employment: A Lifetime Perspective,* HMSO, London.

McGlone F (1992), *Disability & Dependency in Old Age,* Family Policy Studies Centre, London.

Mengani M & Gagliardi C (1993), *Family Care of the Older Elderly: Italy,* Working Paper No. WP/93/26/EN, European Foundation for the Improvement of Living & Working Conditions, Dublin.

Midre G & Synak B (1989), Between Family & State: Ageing in Poland & Norway, *Ageing & Society, 9,* 3.

Morris J (1991), *Pride Against Prejudice,* Women's Press, London.

Naegele G & Reichert M (1993), *Eldercare and the Workplace: A New Challenge for Research & Social Politics,* Paper at British Society of Gerontology Annual Conference, University of Anglia, 17-19 September.

Nissel M & Bonnerjea L (1982), *Family Care of the Handicapped Elderly: Who Pays?,* Policy Studies Institute, London.

Organisation for Economic Co-operation & Development (1988), *Ageing Populations: The Social Policy Implications,* OECD, Paris.

Organisation for Economic Co-operation & Development (1990a), *Urban Policies for Ageing Populations,* Draft Final Report, OECD Group on Urban Affairs ENV/WP/TSDA(90) 1, Paris.

Organisation for Economic Co-operation & Development (1990b), *Urban Policies for Ageing Populations: major Findings & Policy Options,* OECD, Paris.

Organisation for Economic Co-operation & Development (1992), *Urban Policies for Ageing Populations,* OECD, Paris.

Pacolet J, Versieck K & Bouten R (1993), *Social Protection for Dependency in Old Age: Summary of Preliminary Results.* Hoger Instituut voor de Arbeid, Leuven.

Parker G (1993), *Where Next for Research on Carers?* A Think Piece for the Joseph Rowntree Foundation, Nuffield Community Care Studies Unit, University of Leicester, Leicester.

Paukert L (1984), *The Employment & Unemployment of Women in OECD Countries,* Organisation for Economic Co-operation & Development, Paris.

Qureshi H (1986), Responses to Dependency: Reciprocity, Affect & Power in Family Relationships in Phillipson C et al (eds), *Dependency & Interdependency in Old Age,* Croom Helm, London.

Qvortrup J (1989), Comparative Research and its Problems, Chapter One in Boh K, Bak M, Clason C et al, *Changing Patterns of European Family Life,* Routledge, London.

Rabins P V (1985), Promoting Independent Living in a Municipality with 25 Percent Elderly, *Danish Medical Bulletin, Gerontology Special Supplement Series, No 1,* Copenhagen, Denmark.

Reday-Mulvey G (1990), *Work & Retirement: Future Prospects for the Baby-Boom Generation,* The Geneva Papers, No 55, p100-113 (cited in Walker et al 1993).

Rimmer L & Popay J (1982), *Employment Trends & the Family,* Occasional Paper No 10, Study Commission on the Family, London.

Rodriguez J A (1993), *Family Care of the Older Elderly: Spain,* Working Paper No WP/93/23/EN, European Foundation for the Improvement of Living & Working Conditions, Dublin.

Room G (1991), *Towards a European Welfare State?,* School for Advanced urban Studies, University of Bristol, Bristol.

Salvage A (1993), *Heating Controls for Elderly People,* Report for EA Technology Age Concern Institute of Gerontology, King's College, London.

Salvage A V (1986), *Attitudes of the Over 75s to Health and Social Services* Research Team for the Care of the Elderly, University of Wales College of Medicine, Cardiff.

Schou P, Tufte E, Leeson G W (1993), *Family Care of the Older Elderly: Denmark,* Working paper No.WP/93/20/EN European Foundation for the Improvement of Living and Working Conditions, Dublin.

Secretariat for Futures Studies (1978), *Care in Society*, A Project Presentation, Secretariat for Future Studies, Stockholm.

Smallegan M (1983), *How Families Decide on Nursing Home Admission,* Geriatric Consultant, March - April, 21-24.

Smallegan M (1985), *There Was Nothing Else To Do: Needs for care before nursing home admission,* Gerontologist, **25**, 364 - 69.

Steenvorden M A G A (1993), *Family Care of the Older Elderly: The Netherlands,* Working paper No.WP/93/25/EN European Foundation for the Improvement of Living and Working Conditions, Dublin.

Stevenson O (1993), *Informal social care and its implications for formal care,* Chapter Four in Hobman D (ed.).

Sundström G (in press), *Care by Families: An Overview of Trends,* Chapter Two in 'Caring for Frail Elderly People' OECD.

Tinker A (1989), *An Evaluation of Very Sheltered Housing,* HMSO, London.

Tinker A (1991), *Granny Flats - The British Experience* Journal of Housing for the Elderly, **7(2)**, 41-56.

Triantafillou J & Mestheneos E (1993), *Family Care of the Older Elderly: Greece,* Working Paper No.WP/93/16/EN European Foundation for the Improvement of Living and Working Conditions, Dublin.

Twigg J (1990), *Carers of Elderly People: Models for Analysis,* Chapter Two in Jamieson A & Illsley R (eds).

U S Public Health Service (1978), *The Leading Causes of Death in the United States,* Center for Disease Control, Cited in Dooghe, 1992).

Waerness K (1989), Caring, Chapter 11 in Boh K, Bak M, Clason C et al *Changing Patterns of European Family Life*, Routledge, London.

Walker A (1992), *Towards a European Agenda in Home Care for Older People: Convergencies and Controversies* in Evers A and Van der Zanden G (eds) 'Better Care for Dependent People Living at Home', Nijmegen, Netherlands, Institute of Gerontology/European Centre for Social Welfare Policy & Research.

Walker A (1993), *Age and Attitudes: Main Results from a Eurobarometer Survey*, Commission of the European Communities, Directorate General V, Employment, Industrial Relations and Social Affairs.

Walker A, Alber J & Guillemard A-M (1993), *Older People in Europe, Social and Economic Policies. The 1993 Report of the European Observatory.* Commission of the European Communities, Directorate General V, Employment, Social Affairs, Industrial Relations.

West P, Illsley R & Kelman H (1984), Public preferences for the care of dependency groups, *Social Science and Medicine*, 18(4), 287-295.

Wilson G (1993), The challenge of an ageing electorate: changes in the formation of social policy in Europe?, *Journal of European Social Policy*, 3, 91-105.

Work Research Centre/EKOS (1991), *Technology and the Elderly: The Role of Technology in Prolonging the Independence of the Elderly in the Community Care Context.* Work Research Centre/EKOS Social and Environmental Research, Dublin.

Wright F (1986), *Left to Care Alone*, Gower, Aldershot.

Yoxen E (1992), *Home Care: Competitive Goods and Services for Care in the Community*, Centre for Exploitation of Science and Technology, London.

APPENDIX I

NATIONAL REPORTS ON FAMILY CARE FOR OLDER ELDERLY PEOPLE (1993)

B: George Hedebouw
    HIVA - Hoger Instituut voor de Arbeid, Katholieke Universiteit
    E. Van Evenstraat 2E, B-3000 Leuven

D: Hanneli Döhner, Herbert Rüb, Birgit Schick
    Universität Hamburg - Institut für Medizin-Soziologie - Schwerpunkt Sozialgerontologie, Martinistraße 52, D-2000 Hamburg 20

DK: Poul Schou, Eva Tufte, George W Leeson
    EGV - Æeldre Fonden,
    Vesterbrogade 97, DK-1620 København V

E: Josep A Rodriguez-Diaz
    Universidad de Barcelona - Facultad de Econòmicas
    Avda Diagonal 690, E-08034 Barcelona

F: Hannelore Jani-Le Bris
    CLEIRPPA - Centre de Liaison, d'Etude, d'Information et de Recherche sur les Problèmes des Personnes Agées,
    15 rue Chateaubriand, F-75008 Paris

GR: Judith Triantafillou, Elizabeth Mestheneos
    SEXTANT,
    Aktaioy 9A, GR-118 51 Athens

IRL: Joyce O'Connor
     National College of Industrial Relations,
     Sandford Road, Ranelagh, Dublin 6

I: Massimo Mengani, Cristina Gagliardi
    INRCA - Centro Studi Economico-Sociali,
    Scalone S. Francesco n°3, I-60121 Ancona

NL: Mariëtte Steenvoorden
    NIZW Nederlands Instituut voor Zorg en Welzijn,
    Catharijnesingel 47, NL- 3501 DD Utrecht

P: Maria de Lourdes Baptista Quaresma
    Direçao Municipal de Habitaçao Social,
    R. Castilho 213, P-1000 Lisboa

UK: Janet Finch, Richard Hugman
University of Lancaster - Applied Social Science,
Lancaster LA1 4YW

Research Manager: Robert Anderson
European Foundation for the Improvement of Living and Working Conditions

Other studies carried out and published by the Foundation in this series:

Family Care of Dependent Older People in the European Community
(ISBN 92-826-6355-8)
Available in English, French, German, Italian & Spanish

In all countries of the European Community most care and support for older people is provided by their family members, particularly spouses and daughters. This report, based upon literature analyses and interviews with family carers, documents the characteristics of this care, the problems experienced and help received by the carers. It considers what can, and should, be done - by professional carers, voluntary organisation, social partners and the authorities at local, national and European level - to sustain this resource, and to improve the quality of life for family carers.

Carers Talking: Interviews with Family Carers of Older, Dependent People in the European Community
(ISBN 92-826-6570-4)
Available in English & French

Families are, in all EC countries, the cornerstone of care for older people in the community. This volume draws upon interviews with family carers in nine countries to illustrate the daily lives of carers and their attitudes to caring. It illuminates the complexity of care situations, but also underlines the costs - financial, social, emotional and physical - that carers bear.

Family Care of the Older Elderly: Casebook of Initiatives
(ISBN 92-826-6572-0)
Available in English, French & Dutch

Families provide the basic care and support to most older dependent people. The consequent problems and needs of family carers are now, slowly, being recognised in countries of the European Community. This casebook documents initiatives, across the public, private and voluntary sectors, to help and support these family carers of older people.

European Foundation for the Improvement of Living and Working Conditions

Who will care? –
Future prospects for family care of older people in the European Union

Luxembourg: Office for Official Publications of the European Communities

1995 – 98 pp. – 16 x 23,4 cm.

ISBN 92-827-5360-3

Price (excluding VAT) in Luxembourg: ECU 8.50